SANTONA PUBLICATION
2009

SCOTTISH LAYOUT PROJECTS

by
IAN FUTERS

SCOTTISH LAYOUT PROJECTS
First published in 2009
ISBN 978-1-907094-19-4

British Library Cataloguing in Publication Data. A catalogue record for this book is available from the British Library.

Published by: Santona Publications, 382 Carlton Hill, Carlton, Nottingham. NG4 1JA. Santona Publications is an imprint of Book Law Publications, 382 Carlton Hill, Carlton, Nottingham. NG4 1JA.

Printed by the Amadeus Press, West Yorkshire.
Additional information by Steve Flint.
Watercolour artwork by Neil Ripley.
Scale drawings by Peter Goss (Fort William station), A Jay (Rothbury signal box).
Book design and graphics (from the author's originals) by Steve Flint.
Photographs, unless otherwise credited, by the author and Steve Flint courtesy Railway Modeller.
The author and publisher acknowledge the support of Peco Publications and Publicity in the preparation of this book.

Front cover: a photo-montage depicting Fort William station model against a Scottish backdrop.
Title page: urban Scottish railways as portrayed on Victoria Park, an O gauge minimum space layout by the author.

Contents

Part one - Realising the Dream

Part two - Scottish Layout Projects

About the plans in this book.

All plans have been drawn to scale using imperial units. Each square on the grid backgrounds represents 1 sq. ft. Although every attempt as been made to produce the plans as accurately as possible, absolute scale cannot be guaranteed and anyone contemplating building one of them is strongly recommended to carry out their own viability checks with track templates or actual track parts beforehand.

McLEOD
GLEN DOUGLAS
61344
FORT WILLIAM
FOR BALLACHULISH, GLENCOE
AND KINLOCHLEVEN

Dedicated to
Chris Law

Off we go...

Frontispiece: over 35 years of modelling seen in contrast, with B1 No. 61344, on one of my most recent layouts and a central theme to this book - Fort William, whilst (inset) a NBR D34 Glen Class 4-4-0 is seen on one of my earliest layouts - Glen Douglas. The B1 was built by my good friend Stephen Barnfield while the D34 is built from a GEM kit.

PART 1

Realising the Dream

Creating Fort William Station in 7mm scale

We need to go back to 1971 to the time when I had recently finished my teacher-training course on Tyneside and had a few days of my final vacation left. I had purchased a paperback copy of *The West Highland Railway* by John Thomas, and within its pages, noticed a photograph of K1 62034 departing Fort William station in 1952. A small track plan of the terminus seemed to indicate only three platform faces, a couple of turnouts forming the station throat and a crossover linking the bay platforms. I just had to go and see this compact station for myself. I remember booking a return ticket from Newcastle to Berwick upon Tweed along with a seven day Freedom of Scotland rail ticket. Together with a timetable for the whole of Scotland I set off one evening to catch the Kings Cross to Fort William sleeper service, which at that time called in at Newcastle Central at about one o'clock in the morning. With growing excitement, I took my seat in the brake composite coach and headed over the border. I remember little of

the journey that night and feel sure I must not have slept too much. It was a dull morning in Scotland as, with that characteristic Sulzer growl, a Class 27 hauled the sleeper service out though the grey western suburbs of Glasgow and along the north shore of the River Clyde. I remember leaving Craigendoran, the train climbing around the town, then the dramatic change above Loch Long, as the mountain scenery closed in leaving Gareloch and the Clyde behind. The train must have stopped at the lonely platform of Glen Douglas, though I don't recall it: it was an isolated station which I would return to at a later date. Soon after the wooded

surroundings of Ardlui caught my attention: it still remains my favourite station on the whole line. Every tilt and turn of the coach whetted my appetite for more and eventually, when the train crossed Rannoch Moor, I found it difficult to focus on any one spot. There was so much to see and the modelling prospects that it all evoked churned away in my head.

Arrival at Fort William mid-morning saw me straight onto the platforms and away to commence my usual station survey. Black and white photographs were the order of the day then using my trusty Brownie Cresta! Every shot had to count in those days and I still have the negatives taken on that visit: they have been a source of much inspiration for many years. On top of that, I could indeed see that Fort William was quite a cramped station, hemmed in between the town and Loch Linnhe, aloft the sturdy retaining walls which were built to keep the waters of the loch at bay. It was obvious from what I could see that the site would make an ideal model. It had only two turnouts forming the station throat, the crossover between platform two and three had been removed with the onset of the diesels in the 1960s. Quite naturally, a love affair with the Class 27s and their cousins began at the same time.

Thus, back in 1971, the seeds were sown and from that moment I knew that one day I would build a layout depicting Fort William. However, much more research needed to be carried out and although this would

This page and opposite: various views of the station portraying services in and out of Fort William in the early 1950s. Locomotives characteristic of the period include; the ex-LNER K1s (top left), K2s (left and below) and the ex-LMS 5MT 'Black Fives' (above).

have to commence once I had returned to Tyneside, little did I realise it was going to be a further 35 years or so before the project would materialise. There was the little matter of commencing my teaching career and other domestic issues to attend to. Coupled to that was an insatiable interest in the Northumbrian border branch lines which diverted my attention – actually occurring after I had built a couple of West Highland 4mm layouts in 00 gauge A change of gauge to EM and then P4 helped to consolidate my modelling skills but, being closer to my home at that time, the ex-NBR lines within Northumberland became those I tended to concentrate on.

In many respects, that was a great pity. If I had kept true to the West Highland line, I would have perhaps have found out in time that the original Fort William station was to close in 1975 and be replaced by a modern structure further down the line. I didn't, and consequently never did return to the old station: much to my regret too, because now I would

An overall view of the station.The scene clearly shows my preferred approach of generally only modelling up to the railway boundary: by not embarking on great swathes of non-railway scenery, it has allowed me, I believe, the time to build many different layouts over the years.

Above: we certainly like to romanticise about the railway as it used to be, but this early 1970s view of the station shows just what it was like in the real world. There's a general air of neglect with run-down architecture all around, rubbish strewn everywhere and seagulls foraging for left-overs. In platform two can be seen the sleepers and restaurant/buffet car being service in readiness for the outward journey to Kings Cross later that day.

Below: a photo-montage of the station frontage in its later years, C. 1973 and covered in an awful shade of paint.

have to rely upon external sources for research in order to construct the model. Quite early on in my quest I fortunately discovered drawings of the original station building in the BR Public Relations offices in Glasgow. Further information tended to be collected from the prototype magazines of the day. All these were placed in a box file and eventually, a great deal of information was squirrelled away. Plans and photographs, operating notes, timetables, in fact anything relating to West Highland matters all ended up in that box file. I have also acquired a complete list of daily workings in and out of Fort William from Jim Archibald, another good friend, who worked in and around Lochaber as a relief signalman, spending many a day in the town box.

My interest in Fort William was re-awakened in the late 1990s when I was researching the little known line that was proposed to go from

A: Fort William as many a passenger must have seen it. This view shows just how short the platforms were; ideal for modelling of course. A good view of the canopy interiors is also afforded.

B: platform three looking towards the station throat. The frontage on the right dates from the original structure and has clearly seen better days, with many damp patches showing on the paintwork.

C: probably the final incarnation of the station concourse before demolition. Aluminium frames for the shop and office windows suggest a genuine effort to provide modern facilities.

D: the opposite side of the concourse interior, the semi-circular roof lights are shown to good effect in this shot. A strange place for an unattended 'Brute' trolley, perhaps, and what of the milk crates?

Arrochar to St Catherine's by the shores of Loch Fyne. I was horrified to realise how long it had been since I had been to the area. Consequently I commenced photographing the stations on the West Highland line and a series of articles appeared in the *Railway Modeller*. All of this coincided with my move into 7mm scale, although still centred around the Border branches. At the same time, a number of 7mm NBR locomotive kits appeared on the market and this made me think about the possibility of a steam era style layout based in or around the West Highlands. As ever, events were overtaken by a diesel interlude in the Great Glen (Loch Lochy as featured in my previous book) but rolling stock continued to be built, commissioned or purchased, with the final scene in my mind's eye definitely being Fort William.

I was aware that such a project was going to be larger than my normal layout style, despite the usual absence of turnouts as such. I was also aware my locomotive and rolling stock collection would have to be enlarged to include larger locomotives that did not usually have rosters on the Rothbury Branch: after all, any student of the West Highland will appreciate which locomotives operated the line over the years, be they steam or diesel, pre-grouping or British Rail students. Simple issues like the fact coaching stock of other companies other than the LNER (or the NBR) were rarely seen on the line until the advent of the BR Mk 1 coaches, which started to appear from the early 1950s. Another issue that I would have to attend to related to the services found on the West Highland throughout its history, but years of collecting information on the line was to bare fruit at last, though it would take me about ten years to collect or construct much of the stock needed. A start was made whilst I was still in gainful employment, purchasing the kits I would possibly need. This included wagons, coaches and importantly, locomotives. The good old kit cupboard, much loved by modellers, started to groan with the

E: looking towards the concourse. There are clearly some steps leading to an undercroft beneath the station, presumably a storage area of some description.

F: a valuable detail shot of the buffers on platforms two and three. The lever frame is an interesting relic which I believe controlled the release crossover and associated signals.

G: even with a wide angle lens, getting a shot of the road-side elevation was always difficult. The chimney pots, seen in the 1950s view on page 16, are absent by this time.

H: roof detail showing the fan-light at the end of the concourse. Also visible is the destination board which had been modernised by this time to include British Rail standard lettering and colouring.

contents. I aimed to be very selective and only purchased the best. It can be quite easy to be taken in by some unscrupulous traders at some specialist exhibitions and end up purchasing shoddy examples of locomotives in particular! However, as the years progressed, good quality kits started to appear and by the time the layout building commenced, I had many of the items required to operate a basic service. Only a few items remain to be sourced at the time of writing, although I do admit I could do with perhaps two items of some locomotives, but due to finance, one will have to suffice for the time being! Of the items remaining, a good LNER sleeping coach is still required.

I was always sure the key to building Fort William was to commence with the station throat turnouts and then work either side of this central piece. What I ended up with, in order to achieve this, was having the two beautifully curved turnouts built professionally, and then building the first baseboard to place them on. The plan was to follow the course of the sea wall and include the loch, so all the baseboards needed two levels, making construction a lengthy and thoughtful process. Also a compromise on length had to take place and six baseboards were eventually built. The bay platforms can only hold five coaches and not the six coaches as found on the prototype. Three further boards were built to house the hidden sidings, making the length a mighty forty feet or so: slightly larger than my usual layouts!

A fair amount of time was spent ensuring the sea wall looked reasonably correct. Carving each stone individually in plaster looked formidable, so I compromised and used Slaters plastic embossed stone sheets, taking care to do a good job of hiding the joins between each sheet. This was the painted light grey and then the cement course was added by covering every piece in matt white paint. Immediately this was rubbed off with tissue leaving a representation of the cement course where it actually should be. The

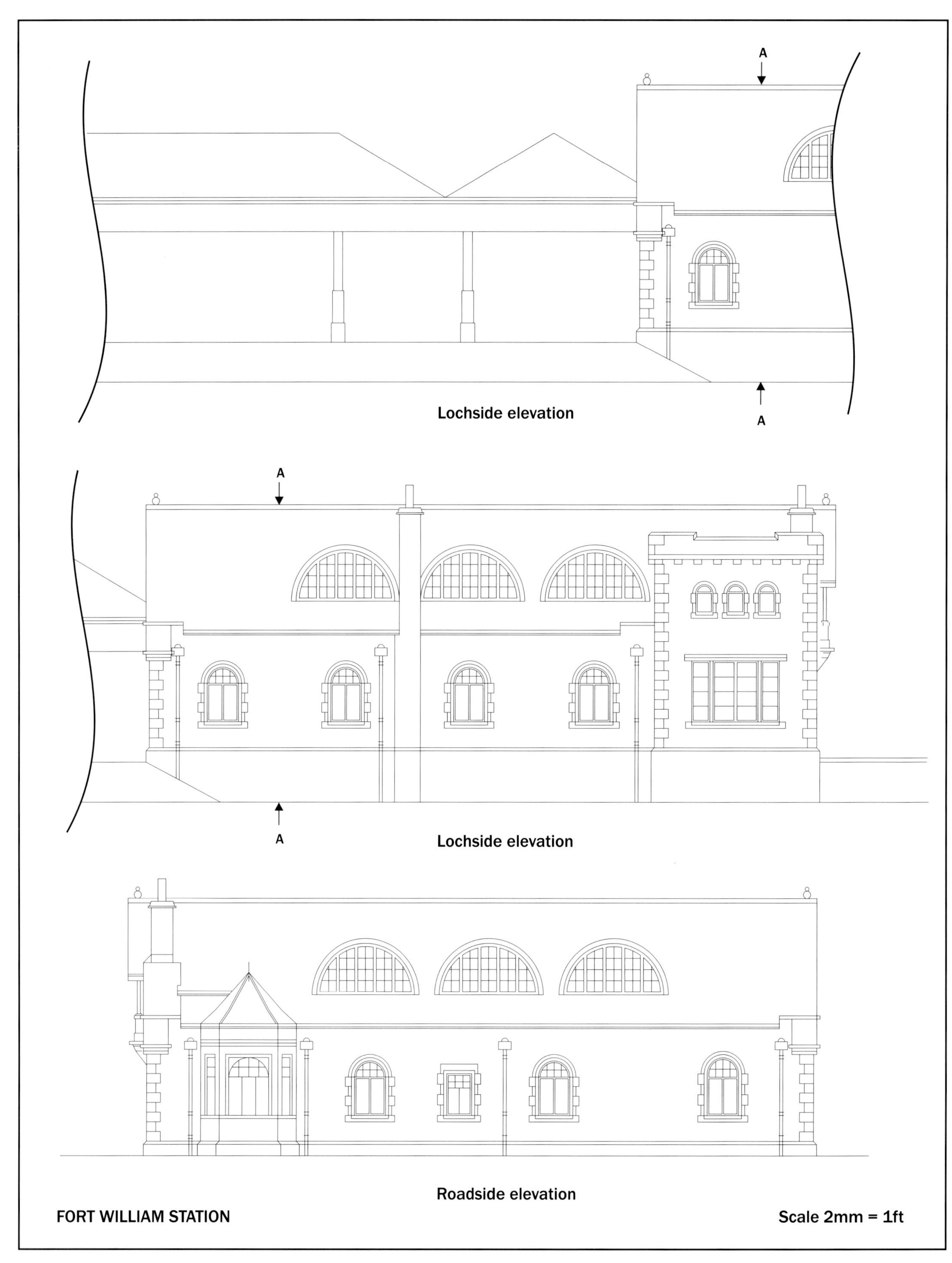
A
A
Lochside elevation
A
A
Lochside elevation
Roadside elevation
FORT WILLIAM STATION
Scale 2mm = 1ft

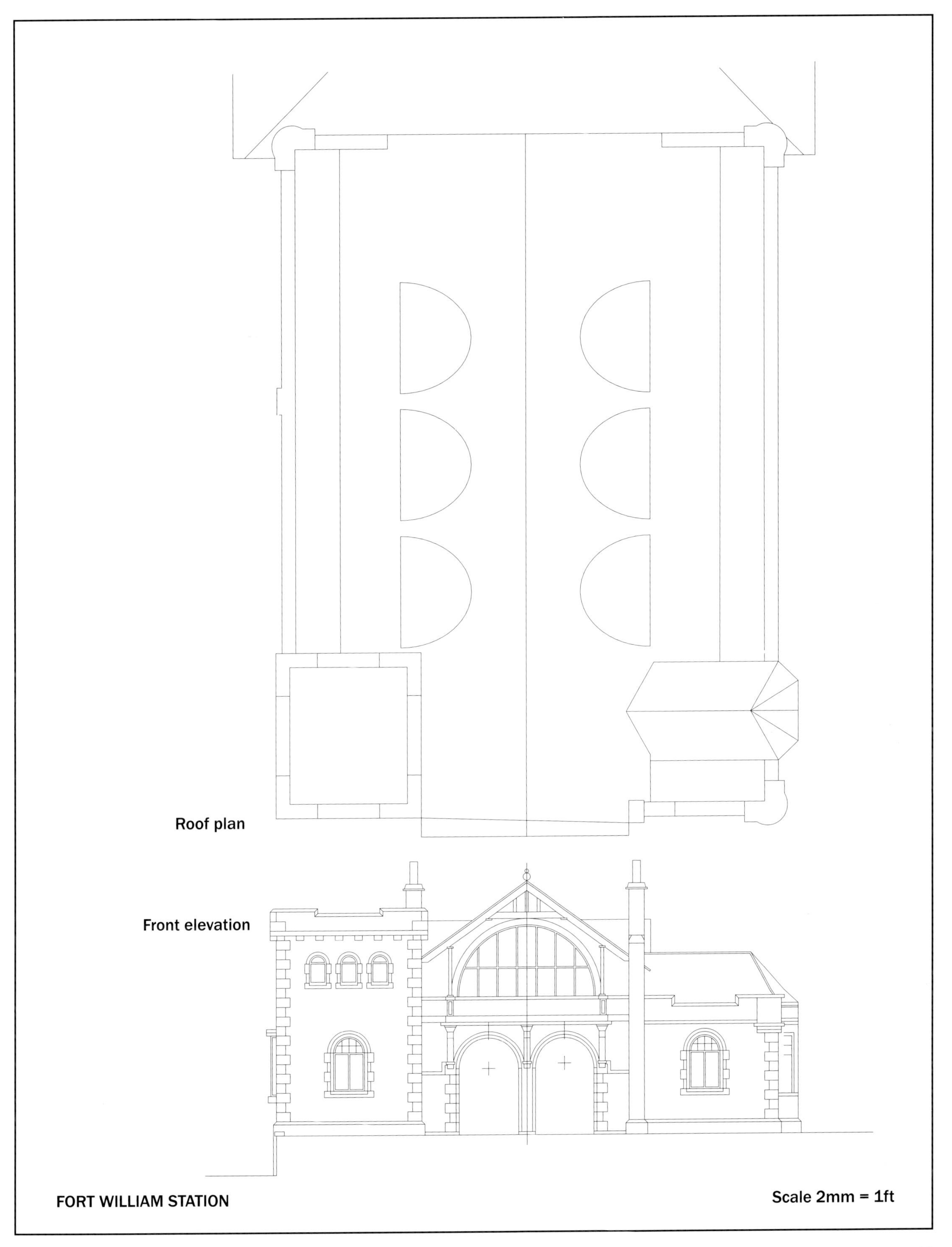
Roof plan
Front elevation
FORT WILLIAM STATION
Scale 2mm = 1ft

Right: a busy station forecourt in the 1950s, the building is seen in original condition. (Photo: author's collection)

bottom edges were dry brushed with various shades of green to represent seaweed clinging to the stones at low tide. I built all the fence posts which ran along the top of the sea wall by hand, although I used etched fencing along the rear of the station site and beside the ash pathway that also ran practically the whole length of the station site, close to the sea wall.

I have, at the moment concentrated on completing the railway structures and only one or two of the buildings outside the station fence. Not long after the station closed a friend of mine took a series of photographs of the buildings which had stood behind the station. These have been extremely useful in assisting the construction of those buildings which stand along the backscene. I was also fortunate in being given a set of slides taken of the railway structures just before the station closed. Some of these accompany this feature, as they are really a historical archive of what used to be. Most of the model structures have been constructed using plywood shells covered with plastic sheet – my usual method. The platform canopies were quite a challenge, but they were unique to the station building and had to be included though I opted out of glazing them because of the sheer size and just painted the tops in a shade of glassy turquoise.

My good friend Derek Mundy produced the magnificent three-doll bracket signals found at the station throat from photographs, modelling them, as requested, as typical NBR lower quadrants. The six signal arms were replaced at sometime with standard British Railways upper quadrant arms so if I eventually operate the station with diesels, I will have to live with that anomaly.

The town signal box controlled all the movements within Fort William station confines. All trains arriving required a station pilot to remove all the service coaching stock and either place it in another platform, or take empty coaching stock to the yard. The incoming locomotive would then return to the depot to be serviced and turned.

If the train was a Glasgow through service to Mallaig, (or the return Mallaig-Glasgow) instead of shunting the stock to release the locomotive, a replacement train engine would drift back into the station to couple up and await the signal to depart, afterwards the incoming locomotive would then be released to the yard. In between all of this, a station pilot (usually a J36) would be bustling about, moving coaches around. The sleeper coaches and buffet or restaurant coaches would be removed from the early morning arrival and placed in the bay platforms to await their return services south in the evening. Even freight arrivals and departures ventured up to the town box, as they all had to either receive or hand over a token before commencing further. So despite the cramped conditions, quite a busy scene should be possible given the availability of the various items rolling stock.

However, and it is a big however, I have had to compromise on the stock available. It would be a very expensive ambition to collect all the necessary stock required. I already had most of the typical freight stock, including a quantity of fish vans, thus, a daily freight service, and even a daily fish working, was possible. Where I really needed to concentrate my efforts was on the main line locomotive and stock roster. In the final analysis, I decided to use a 'minimum' passenger service consisting of one full Glasgow – Fort William/Mallaig working. This would comprise of five coaches which had to double-up up as both morning arrival and evening departure services. A further two coach rake would be the mid-morning and afternoon Mallaig – Fort William – Mallaig local services. Thus a minimum of seven coaches would be needed, made up of Gresley and Thompson stock with perhaps a BR Mk1 brake third. For the period they are in carmine and cream livery, though a teak finished Gresley would be nice to ring the changes.

Much of this stock is now in use: the sleeping coach is still missing, but the Gresley Buffet is now ready for shunting off the morning arrival. Hopefully, other vehicles will be constructed in future so further sets can be made up for variety. I also have a small selection of parcels stock, which are added to the services as required. Naturally, the odd fish van can be attached too: who can tell whether they are full or empty? On the freight side, I will be including the LNER Alumina wagons used on the Fort William – Burntisland route.

As I mentioned earlier, the locomotive stud was built up using a variety of kits. A number of the locomotives have been built by master builder Stephen Barnfield, who just happens to be yet another good friend of mine. He has put together a K2 2-6-0, a B1 4-6-0, a Black Five 4-6-0 and the trusty station pilot, a J36 0-6-0. Other locomotives include a K1, K1/1 and a K4 along with a D34 Glen 4-4-0.

In the 'shops' are a further Glen and two 0-6-0s; a J35 and a J37. A Gresley J39 can be called upon, along with a C15 4-4-2, although by the time of my chosen period (1953), they were rarely seen on the line, being associated much more with the earlier LNER period.

I feel quite sure that the diesels will make an appearance - as below- if all goes well. I prefer the blue 1970s period, so there should be an assortment of Class 27s along with the odd Class 20, 24, 25 and 29. No doubt my Class 08 shunter 08 718, will perform the role of station pilot. The coaching stock will probably be exclusively Mk1 stock, although there could be an ex-LNER Diagram 167 buffet car too. Much of the current freight stock will be suitable as well, along with some British Rail GUV and CCT parcels stock. Like the steam locomotives, suitable diesel 7mm locomotives are readily available, either in kit form, or as Lima conversions. Suitable British Railways Mk1 and Mk2 coaches, as well as NPCCS are available too. It has taken me a number of years to achieve this availability in 7mm, but as I mentioned in my first book, there never has been a better time to commence modelling Scottish prototypes in whatever scale. Even in 4mm thanks to Heljan (and others) such well known Scottish prototypes are now available, though devotees of N Gauge have a little more 'catching up' to do.

My model of Fort William has already been seen on the exhibition circuit at a few selected shows as this book reaches the shelves, and it was not without an amount of trepidation that I launched it - the largest layout (in terms of physical size) that I have ever built.

As I write this section, a number of issues have still to be resolved; mainly with the back scene, etching and uncoupling departments. Given time, I am sure they will be solved. After all, that is half the fun of this hobby, dealing with challenging issues - even if they do create headaches from time to time.

Unfortunately my launch of Fort William was blighted by fate: Steve Corrigall, my trusty operator and close friend for many years, was taken ill shortly before the layout's debut at the 2008 Glasgow Show.

A long recovery period has been necessary and although other friends have been able to help from time to time, later in 2008 I took the decision to withdraw Fort William from the exhibition circuit. In the meantime I wish Steve a speedy recovery.

So, that concludes a brief description about how my 'Magnum Opus' project came about. Now let us have a closer look at some further projects, which I would like to think, will offer inspiration to others as modelling projects. Perhaps, when Fort William has done its time, I might tackle some myself.

Thus, in writing this second book I hope it will stimulate other modellers to consider building layouts of railways within the boundaries of Scotland, past or present. It must be said, I have yet again strayed over the Border into my native Northumberland, but despite that, or perhaps inclusive of that, I have to ask who can really resist the variety of railways that run amongst the wonderful land of mountain, moor and loch that we all know as Scotland?

Although out of period for Fort William as portrayed, the opportunity to run Class 27s with blue and grey Mk1 coaches has been irresistible.

Lochend

A just-supposing Highland Railway terminus

I produced a small P4 layout with this title in the mid 1980s, although it was based on North British Railway practice. I chose the name simply to carry on my tradition of having the word 'Loch' somewhere in the station name. At the time I was unaware that a small village, close to the very northern shores of Loch Ness, had the same name and was to be connected to the Highland Railway network at the end of the nineteenth century. It was probably in connection with the 1896 Light Railways Act that a company proposed to build a light railway from Inverness to the head of Loch Ness, a distance of about eight miles. The new branch would leave the Far North line a short distance west of Inverness station, close I assume to Clachnaharry, before heading in a south westerly direction to Lochend. It would pass the small settlement of Dunain on its way and close to a hospital complex at Charleston: perhaps even a small hospital railway could have also existed at that location. A halt would have been planned to serve the settlement at Dochgarroch, where the canal and river part company.

It would appear that the proposing company had no particular connection with the Highland Railway, it simply wanted to improved communications

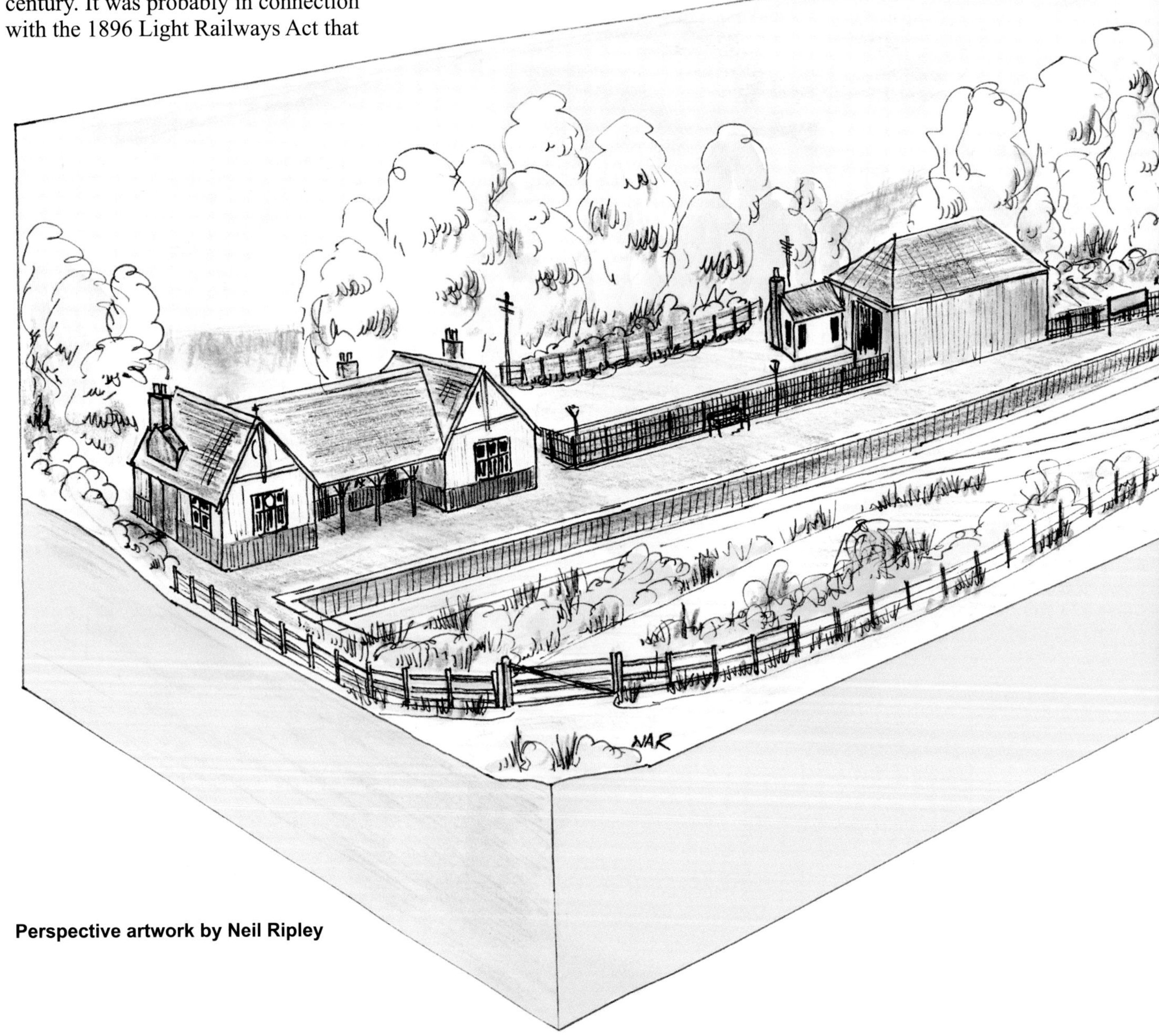

Perspective artwork by Neil Ripley

within the Great Glen, Fort Augustus and thence, Fort William. The fact that no junction had been planned with the Highland Railway, or indeed issues regarding as to who was to operate the line, ensured that the line was never authorised by the Light Railway Commissioners. Of course, the Invergarry and Fort Augustus Railway Company had their say too, and objected most strenuously, as they usually did, despite their own line not opening until 1903. One has to conclude, that the tiny I&FAR were probably the main reason in the end why a through route to Inverness was never constructed. They remained a very territorial company, and it eventually proved their downfall.

However, let us assume the line was completed and a small terminus station was built at the head of Loch Ness. I have reason to believe, by the careful observation of maps and actual on-site surveys, the terminus would not have been close to either Loch Ness or the tiny Loch Dochfour and Abbey Water, which are at the head of Loch Ness itself. Also, the River Ness and the Caledonian Canal head towards Inverness and the coast, more or less parallel to each other for five miles or so and at some point, the railway would have had to cross the canal, but I suspect that this would have possibly been closer to

Lochend at a glance

Design Scale:	**4mm and 7mm.**
Location:	**North end of Loch Ness just south of Inverness.**
Period:	**1950s - 1970s; though could be backdated.**
Size of Layout:	**4mm - 7ft x 1ft 6ins.**
Motive Power:	**BR 4MT, 2MT, McIntosh 0-4-4T, CR Jumbo 0-6-0 Diesel Classes; 08, 21, 24, 26.**
Typical Traffic:	**Branch passenger service, possibly as a daily mixed train. Freight wagons for; coal, general merchandise, fuel oil, finished timber, livestock, agricultural produce, bagged fertiliser.**

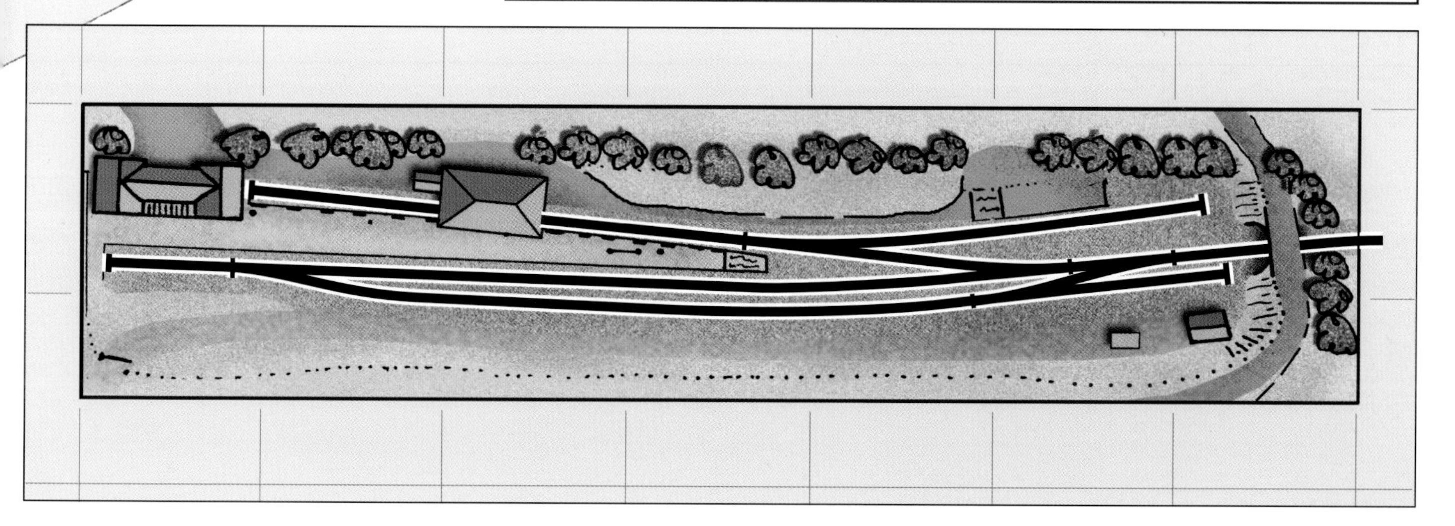

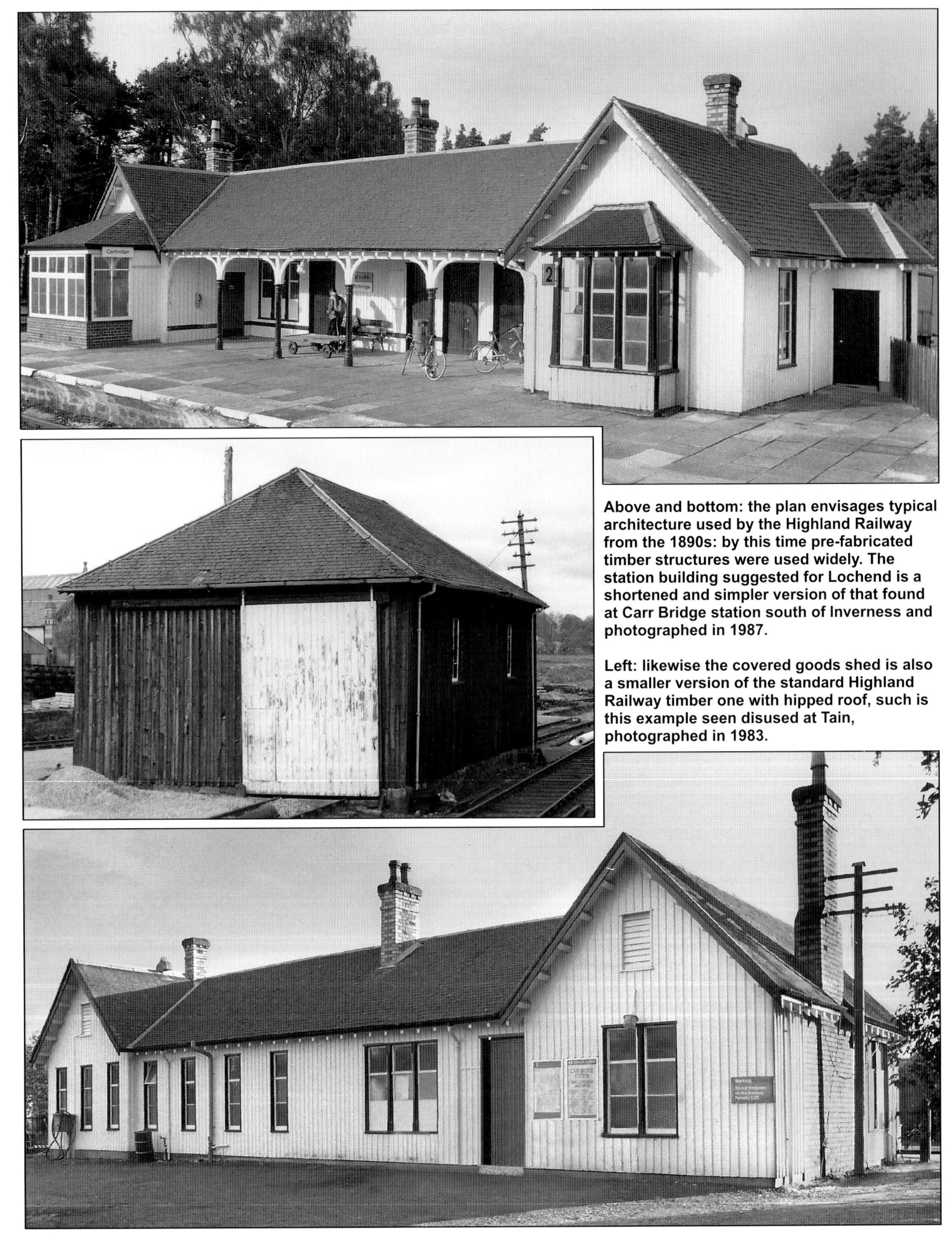

Above and bottom: the plan envisages typical architecture used by the Highland Railway from the 1890s: by this time pre-fabricated timber structures were used widely. The station building suggested for Lochend is a shortened and simpler version of that found at Carr Bridge station south of Inverness and photographed in 1987.

Left: likewise the covered goods shed is also a smaller version of the standard Highland Railway timber one with hipped roof, such is this example seen disused at Tain, photographed in 1983.

Clachnaharry. Further the land behind Lochend, and the A82, rises steeply within a wooded area, though there is just enough land to fit a small terminus station in at this point, so, no water and no bridges on this plan. Naturally, as this is a 'just supposing' style of layout, it could be moved closer to the canal itself if desired, but a little further on where the canal widens out into the Mairtown Basin which, no doubt in the past, was a sort of exchange area for goods traffic.

The design is slightly larger than my original *Lochend* layout (below), which only consisted of a loop and one siding that served a loading bank and a short bay platform. Here, I have added an additional siding, for operational interest along with a smaller style Highland Railway wooden planked goods shed and a small kick-back siding serving a cattle dock. No locomotive facilities are provided, as the branch was only eight miles or so from Inverness depot itself, though there would possibly have been watering facilities at the station for steam locomotives.

The layout is also designed to fit on quite narrow boards, possibly no more than 18" wide in 4mm scale as shown, and could be down-sized to about 2' wide in 7mm scale.

The two baseboards would be 3' 6" long each in 4mm scale but would need to be proportionally longer in 7mm scale, otherwise the whole scene may appear too cramped. I would suggest 12' would be a practical size in the senior scale. A set of hidden sidings would naturally be required and could take the form of a sector plate or a cassette system. Taking into account the train lengths required for the layout, no more than four feet would be required for this facility.

Setting the layout within the pre-grouping period would be a challenging exercise, but would possibly suit an experienced modeller who is comfortable building white metal or etched kits. The LMS period could also be interesting, with a greater use perhaps of ready-to-run equipment. I feel sure there would be nothing to stop anyone sending an Inverness based Black Five down the branch either. The early British Railways period would also see similar motive power, but what about imagining the line remained open until the 1960s. Highly unlikely, but hey! Whose layout is it? The Sulzer Bo-Bo Type 2 locomotives; beautiful machines in my eyes - as I so often relate; started to appear in the Highlands from about 1961 and had more or less taken over most of the services within two years or so. The Heljan Class 26 falls into this category of course, and if we are honest, what a godsend Heljan has been to Scottish Modellers! A Bachmann Class 24 or 25 would not look out of place either, whilst being so close to Inverness, a short freight hauled by a Class 08 would be a distinct possibility too.

Finally, and really as an afterthought, I would suggest this small project could be made into a slightly larger version of my original 'Ashleigh' layout that I built and exhibited way back in 1972. By using small radius Peco pointwork I think the scheme might just squeeze down onto one 5' baseboard. A small hidden siding board would need to be added for the run off. I'm also tempted to say, it could be completed within a week, just like 'Ashleigh' was.

Well, what are you waiting for?

The original Lochend

Built in the 1980s to EM gauge, my original *Lochend* layout seen here consisted of just a loop and one bay siding. It was based on the terminus at Lochty in Fife and set firmly in ex-North British Railway territory in the 1950s. More details can be found in my earlier book *Modelling Scotland's Railways*.

Cromarty

The Highland Railway terminus that got away

Just north of Inverness, there lies a peninsula between the Beauly and Cromarty Firths. The locality has rich farming land and in the past, a flourishing fishing industry around Fortrose, in the south. At the northernmost tip of the peninsula, overlooking Nigg Bay, is the main town, Cromarty. The peninsula itself has a particularly dark name, being called the Black Isle, although this perhaps has more to do with colour of the soil rather than a mysterious past. During the nineteenth century, when the iron rails were being pushed northwards from Inverness, the Black Isle was looked upon as being rather isolated, and as a result, was not placed on the railway maps of the time. The nearest railhead was actually Muir of Ord on the main route to Wick and Thurso.

In order to serve the locality, and in particularly the fishing industry in the south, a railway was eventually proposed from Muir of Ord to Rosemarkie, a distance of nearly sixteen miles. By February 1894 the railway was opened as far as Fortrose. The short extension of one mile to Rosemarkie itself was never completed. Despite this railway, it was still quite a journey via Muir of Ord to Inverness. A shorter route could have been built, but it would have required an expensive bridge at Kessock Ferry, just opposite Inverness, across the Beauly Firth itself.

What happened next was quite amazing, and forms the basis of what I am calling the Cromarty Branch. A similar occurrence happened in Northumberland when a small branch was proposed to a tiny fishing village called Seaton Sluice, just north of Whitley Bay. That line was proposed and actually built by the North Eastern Railway, but it never opened. It was more or less completed just as the Great War commenced in 1914. As a result of the war effort, the rails were all lifted and despite the plans being reincarnated by the LNER in the early 1920s, it was never opened. The same thing, believe it or not, happened on the Black Isle during the formative years of the twentieth century.

Under the auspices of the 1896 Light Railways Act, a line was proposed to reach Cromarty from the county town at Dingwall, home also of Ross County Football Club by the way. It was to follow the northern coast line via Cullicudden. There was to be a rather large and therefore, expensive bridge over the River Conan at Alcraig Ferry. The Light Railway Commissioners would not permit this route and insisted that the junction on the main line should be further south at Conan. The Light Railway Act was obtained in 1902, but as yet, the proposed routes were still not finalised. Further delays in obtaining land meant that time extensions were twice asked for until eventually construction commenced, not at the junction with the Highland main line, but from the Cromarty end.

Roughly six miles of trackwork were actually laid with the earthworks prepared for a further two miles, as far as Cullicudden itself, when war broke out in 1914. Like the project in Northumberland, the rails were lifted shortly afterwards for use elsewhere. The project was never completed after the Great War despite some bridges and culverts being in place, and earthworks still prepared. There was a further eleven miles to be started, and perhaps that, and the forthcoming 'Grouping' of the railways into four major companies, was a contributing factor in the line never being completed. The world economy was also unsteady during the post-war period, and monies would have been in short supply.

It leaves us, as modellers, with a perfect example of a Scottish branch line, just crying out to be completed, in model form of course. The branch would have curved north eastwards from Conan station and headed three miles or so along the Cromarty Firth coastline to Alcraig. A typical Highland Railway single platform halt with a short siding and loading bank would have sufficed at this small village. Hugging the coast to avoid the Millbuie Hills (550ft –650ft), the line at this point would have been relatively easy to construct with no gradients of note to worry about. There are a number of tiny settlements along the coast and there could well have been a single platform halt at Culbokie or the quaintly named Shoretown, but by now the line is climbing steadily towards Drumcudden and Cullicudden. Laurie Griffiths once built a P4 layout named *Cullicudden* and operated as a strict Highland Railway branch line.

By now the route would have skirted past Balblair, where a ferry went across the Firth to Invergordon on the opposite shore. Keeping fairly

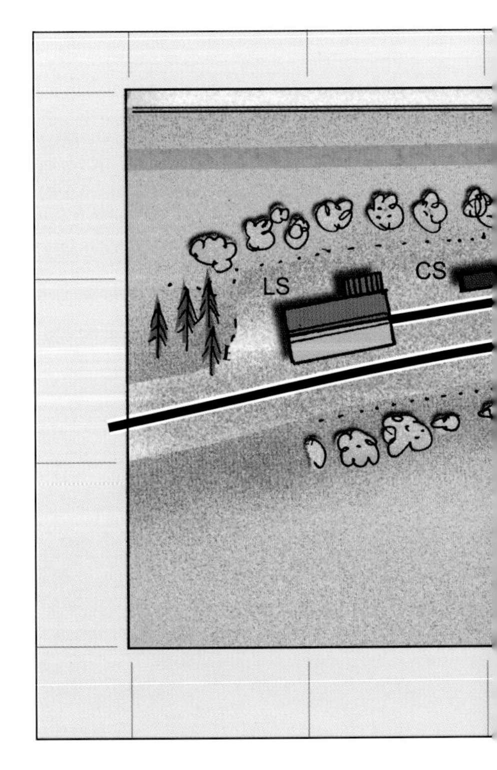

close to the shore, the small settlement of Jemimaville is passed, quite a whimsical station name that would have been, and of course at this stage, we are actually following the original course of the line. Four miles further on and the terminus at Cromarty is reached. The line would have been about 19 miles long and single track. Cullicudden would have been roughly half way between Conan and Cromarty, so there may have been a passing loop there. Any other stations or halts would have been simply a platform with possibly a single siding and loading bank.

Typical wooden board and batten station buildings in the Highland style would have sufficed at these halts, although a more substantial 'H' style station building, would have been found at the terminus, probably identical in style, but larger than that proposed for the previous layout scheme *Lochend*. Also there would have been a timber goods shed and possibly a small engine shed, possibly even a small turntable too, but as small HR tank locomotives would have operated the services, much like the Dornoch branch, described later in this book, such an expensive feature would have been dispensed with.

The Fortrose branch closed to passenger traffic on 1st October 1951. There were two trains daily with an additional service on Saturdays. That would have sufficed on the Cromarty branch too. Freight services lasted until June 1960 on the Fortrose line, just before the diesels arrived in the locality. There would be no harm in stretching the closure period to cover the use of the Type 2 diesel types, in early green livery of course. As it was built under the Light Railway Act, quite a simple station would have been constructed, and one which could be made much smaller than the plan suggests.

Much of the Highland or LMS steam stock would have to be kit-built, but one or two ready-to-run items could be sourced. Altogether, quite a basic but practical layout, and one which could well suit a young or novice modeller who wishes to utilise his Hornby or Bachmann trackwork.

Cromarty at a glance

Design Scale:	**4mm.**
Location:	**County town located on the Black Isle.**
Period:	**Pre-grouping through to 1970s to suit.**
Size of Layout:	**10ft x 3ft, though could easily be made smaller.**
Motive Power:	**Highland or Caledonian McIntosh 0-4-4Ts, CR Jumbo 0-6-0, BR 4MT standard tanks. Diesel Classes; 21, 24, 25, 26.**
Typical Traffic:	**Branch passenger again possibly as a daily mixed train. Freight wagons for; coal, general merchandise, machinery, fish, livestock, fuel.**

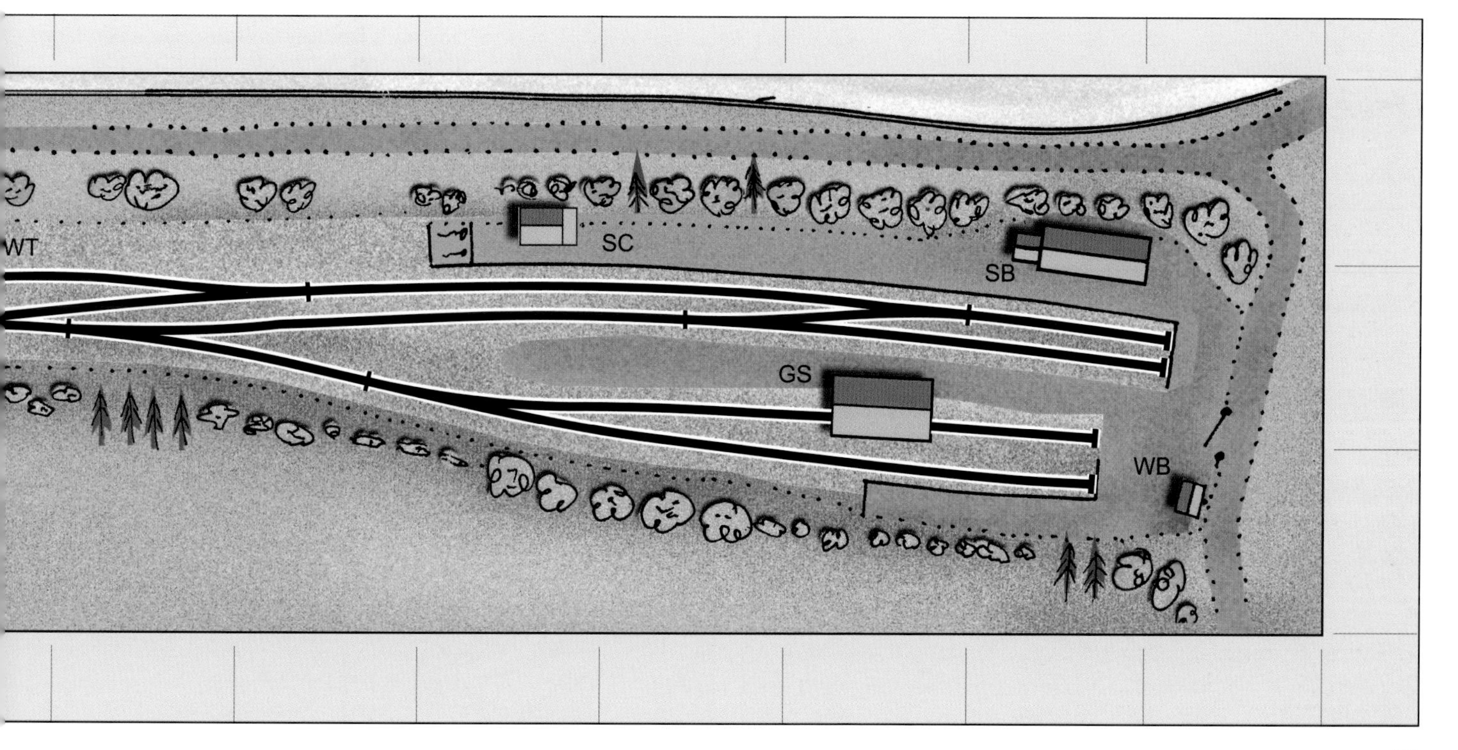

The Dornoch Branch

A room sized layout for main line and branch running

Throughout Scotland, there could once be found branch lines which are compact enough to be described in full and modelled in their entirety. In my first book, I suggested the branches to Eyemouth and Moffat could be approached in this way. Another such example is the Dornoch branch that ran from a junction station called The Mound on the Highland Railway's Far North line.

The branch served the county town of Dornoch which, because of its location on the northern shore of the Dornoch Firth, had been by-passed by the railway network in the 1870s. The main line had to head inland from Tain and make a huge detour via Lairg before heading back eastward towards the coast and Golspie.

The Highland Railway agreed with the promoters towards the end of the 19th C. that Dornoch should be linked to the outside world and a short seven and three quarter mile single-track branch line was proposed. The line was to follow closely Thomas Telford's original road to Dornoch built across a causeway over Loch Fleet in 1817. The railway became known as the Dornoch Light Railway, having been built under the Light Railways Act of 1896. This allowed the promoters to build their line with lighter section rail and dispense with a full signalling scheme. Some light railway lines were allowed to leave their line unfenced but the Dornoch line was fully fenced and had gates at the main road crossings.

The line was authorised on the 13th August 1898 and took four years to complete, opening on 2nd June 1902. Throughout its lifetime, one class of locomotive was associated with the branch: Peter Drummond's diminutive Highland Railway 0-4-4T class of 1905. They served the branch right up until 1957 when the last example was withdrawn because of problems to one of its axles. Most unusually, for the final three years of the line's existence (it closed completely on the 13th June 1960) two ex-GWR Pannier tank locomotives were drafted in to operate the services. These two locomotives,

Dornoch Station Building: as seen from the station yard (left) and from the north end (below left) in 1990. The platform side seen in use in 1959 (below right) with former GW Pannier No. 1646 arriving with a mixed train (photo: Douglas Hume).

apparently, were light weight enough to run on the lightly built route. Of course, that always makes an excellent quiz question for any railway club's Christmas quiz: what, where and why did GWR locomotives regularly work in Scotland?

The junction at The Mound was quite a simple affair, with a loop on the main line itself and a further loop alongside the branch platform. Both formed a slightly triangular track plan. Sidings serving loading banks were located both off the main line and the branch. The River Fleet passed directly in front of the junction site as it flowed into Loch Fleet: the branch heading across the causeway and over four short, but distinctive, girder bridges as it skirted the southern shores of the loch. A small halt was located here to serve the hamlet of Cambusavie, whilst a small station was found near to Skelbo. This was very close to the peninsula whereby the waters from Loch Fleet flowed into the North Sea and where a ferry used to link this piece of land with Littleferry on the opposite shore. The railway then followed the coastline through to Dornoch itself, passing a further intermediate station at Embo. Both Skelbo and Embo had the usual small Highland Railway wooden planked station building, a siding and

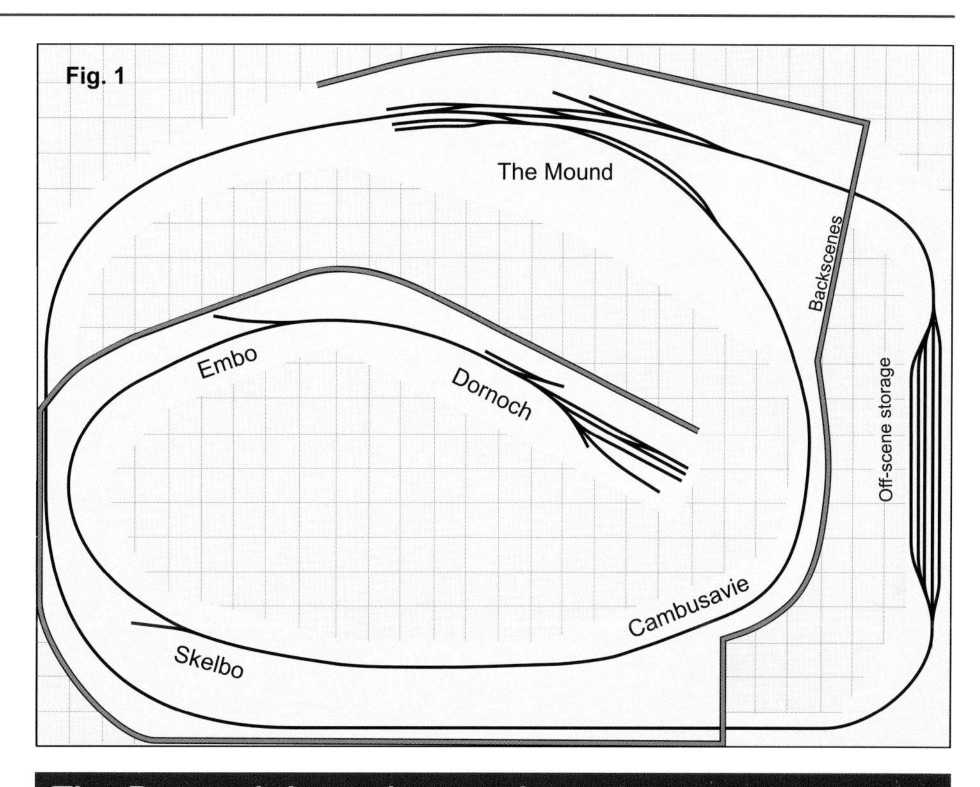

The Dornoch branch at a glance

Design Scale:	**4mm, an N gauge version is certainly possible.**
Location:	**Easter Ross, north east Scotland.**
Period:	**Pre-grouping through to 1960.**
Size of Layout:	**Various, depending on which station modelled, a smaller version of Dornoch could be built as shown highlighted on plan below.**
Motive Power:	**Highland classes or Black Fives on the main line, Drummond 0-4-4T, CR McIntosh 0-4-4Ts or GW 16xx on the branch.**
Typical Traffic:	**Mixed service, coal and general merchandise.**

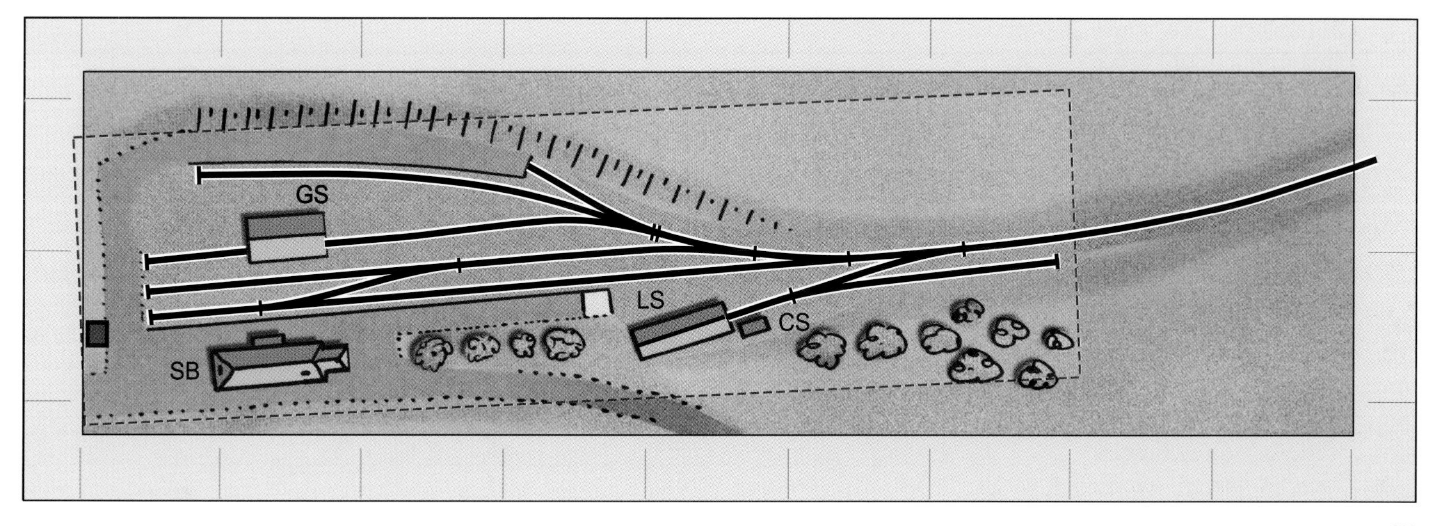

a loading bank, both locations also had gated crossings. Two miles from Embo the diminutive terminus at Dornoch was reached.

As the trains arrived at Dornoch, a spur to the left led to an engine shed, with a short kick-back siding alongside the main running track. Basically that was it: an extremely compact branch terminus laid with light-weight rail unchanged up to its closure. The station could easily be built as a stand-alone project, or made to fit into a more generous scheme as seen in Fig 1. on page 25. The room scheme includes the three intermediate stations, The Mound junction, (all illustrated right) and a stretch of main line for through running. It is based on the details of each station shown in the larger scale plans. What strikes me about the scheme is the size - 29' x 20' - though I'm sure it could be condensed a little, with tighter radii etc., but at least full length trains, both branch and main line ones, could be operated prototypically as a 1950s period scheme, or backdated, to Highland Railway or LMS periods.

The project uses Dornoch as a centre piece and has the rest of the branch plus the junction around the walls of the room. Also included is a stretch of the Far North main line around the perimeter as seen in Fig. 1. It is presented as visible behind and parallel to the branch, a format that is unusual to UK modellers, but popular in the States.

Alternatively you could just choose to do Dornoch itself as a portable layout suitable for exhibition use and I would imagine it could be squeezed into a smallish space, possibly eight or nine feet. A smaller version (shown dotted) is presented if wide baseboards are not to your liking.

There is a useful booklet available from the Highland Railway Society entitled, *The Dornoch Branch.* This small volume by Barry C. Turner (ISBN 0 9513358 1 2) will give you most of the information you require including views of the goods shed and more of the station building.

As I have indicated, the branch was operated for many years with the HR 0-4-4T locomotives, and certainly during the early 1950s, the passenger train consisted of either 55051 or 55053 along with a single Stanier main-line brake composite vehicle in 'blood and custard' livery (SC 6730M or SC 6743M I think). However, a LMS non-corridor was photographed on the service in 1959. Mixed trains were the norm on the branch, with one or two fish vans of LNER or BR

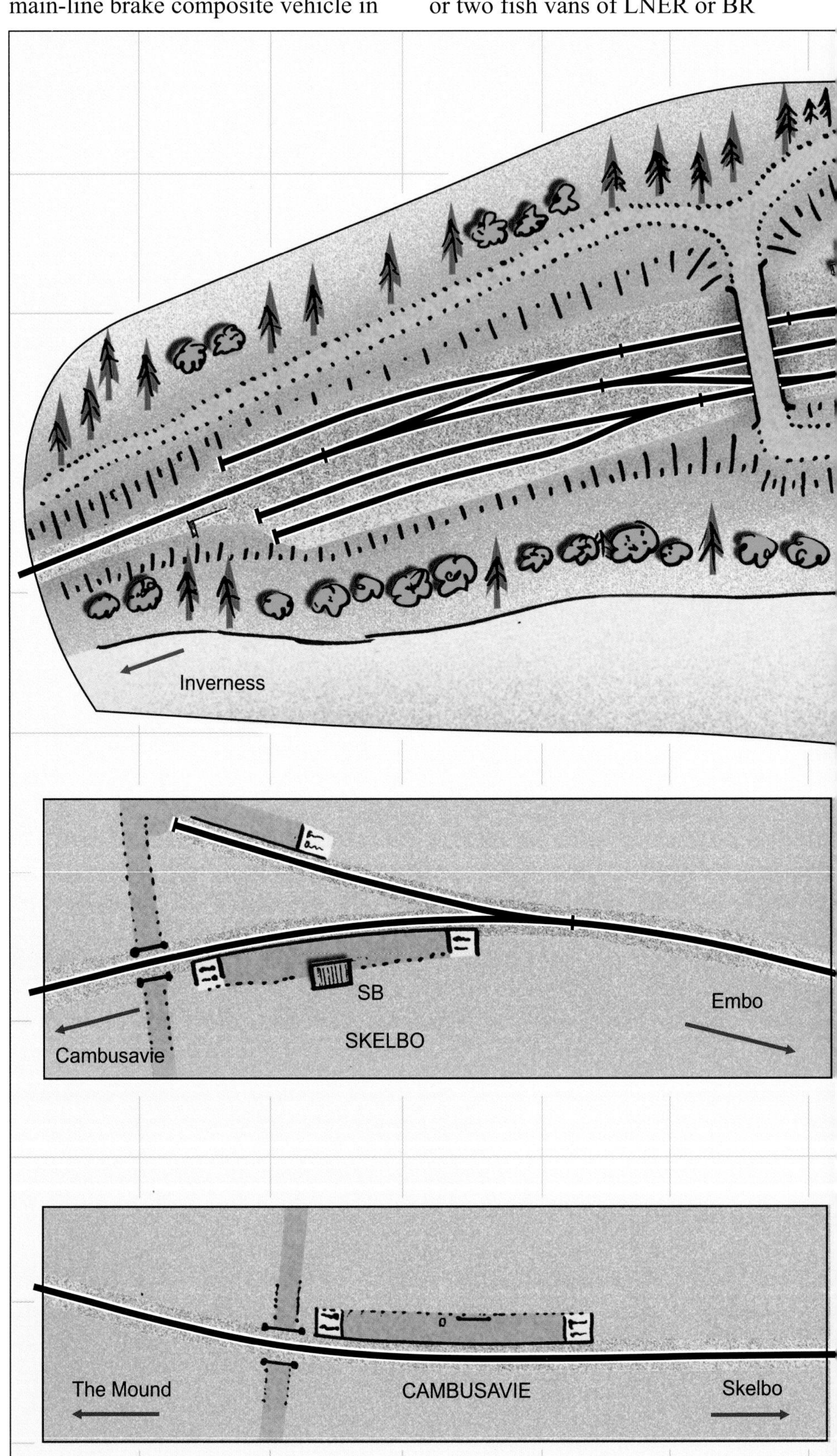

vintage seen, as well as the usual vans and open wagons. Of the two ex-GWR pannier tanks sent north in 1957 belonging to the 1600 Class, No. 1646 appears often in photographs, the other pannier tank available was 1649. Prior to these locomotives working the line, and about the time of the withdrawal of the two Highland Railway locomotives, Caledonian 0-4-4T, No. 55236, complete with its distinctive stove-pipe chimney was observed. Also of note for the modeller contemplating a fine scale version using handbuilt track: interlaced timbering on pointwork was still to be seen in the 1950s, and probably up until closure.

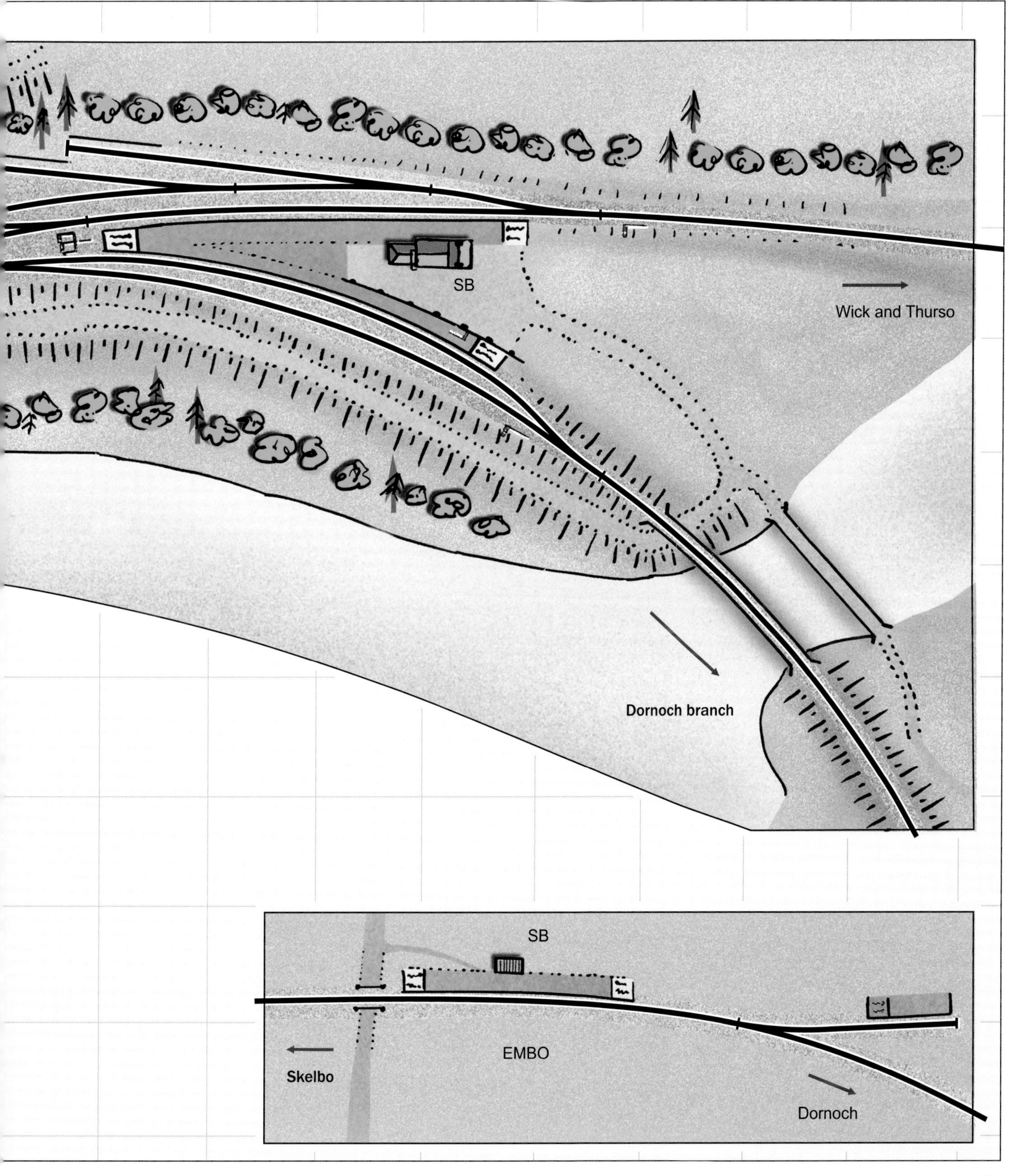

Kyle of Lochalsh

A plan for this famous terminus in the western highlands

The lone piper plays a haunting lament, weak autumn sunshine glances over the dancing waves of Loch Alsh. Above the distant peaks of the Cuillin Hills, dark and menacing storm clouds are gathering. That can be the very view you can see from perhaps one of the most celebrated and romantic Highland railway stations still operational. It is of course the view from the old Highland Railway's distant outpost at Kyle of Lochalsh. Even today, the journey from Inverness along the Dingwall and Skye line is an adventure as it is one of the most isolated lines in Scotland. Nevertheless, at least it is still possible to experience the spectacular scenery along the route, whilst the view from the end of the platform looking across the loch is awesome, in whatever weather happens to be around at the time!

The Kyle line, as it became known, was opened as far as Strome Ferry in 1870. It was to be a further 27 years before the terminus at Kyle of Lochalsh was reached, in 1897. The usual financial reasons as well as difficult engineering works were the main reason for the delay, but as the Highland Railway entered the 20th century, they at least had a more suitable harbour for their railway, as well as a closer link to the islands nearby. It would be a further eighty years or so before the mainland was eventually linked to the Isle of Skye, with the much maligned toll road bridge. Fortunately, common sense

Top right: the scene in 1986 as 37 418 runs around the morning arrival. The area to the right had all track lifted sometime between 1981 and 1984.

Right: a new siding parallel to the quayside appears to have been taken over by the locals in this 2005 view.

Opposite: also seen in 2005, the station building much as it was 100 years ago.

has prevailed, and the exorbitant charges have been revoked. Perhaps one day it may be interesting to look at the proposed itineraries of the Highland Railway to construct narrow gauge lines on the Isle of Skye itself, more or less at the same time the final miles to Kyle of Lochalsh were being completed, a fascinating thought, especially for narrow-gauge modellers in particular.

Kyle of Lochalsh at a glance

Design Scale:	**Main scheme: 4mm. Shed scheme: 7mm.**
Location:	**North west Scotland.**
Period:	**1980 - present day though ripe for backdating**
Size of Layout:	**see grid scaling on relevant plan.**
Motive Power:	**Main scheme: Classes 37, 67 and 156, 158 units Shed scheme: any diesel types to suit.**
Typical Traffic:	**Daily passenger workings, occasional locomotive hauled specials such as the *Hebridean Heritage* or *Royal Scotsman.* Some freight and engineers' traffic.**

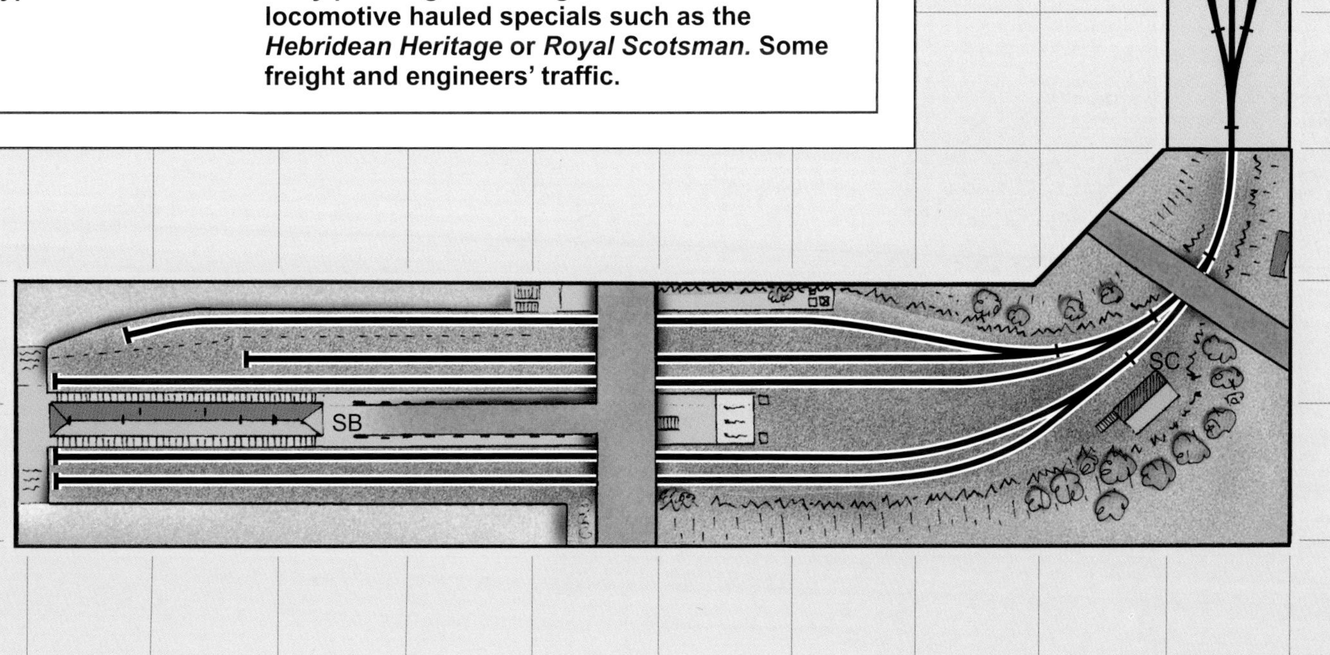

When you observe the terminus at Kyle today, it has not changed much since those far off days, over a hundred years ago. The same long island platform is in use, as is the ramp sloping from the main road bridge which crosses the station site. The platform roads are still in place of course, complete with a run-round loop, and the line still curves away beautifully at the station throat, just along from the traditional Highland signal cabin, standing resolute like a sentinel. The rather long loading dock, which would have perhaps been used for cattle as well as fish, is still intact, but the plethora of sidings, have all gone, though only within the last 25 years or so. The station building is quite a length, complete with its canopies, and that too dates back to Highland days. Nowadays, the Friends of the Kyle line have a display within the station building as well as a small gift shop. Much of the trackwork was not removed until the advent of Class 37 operations in the early 1980s, so if modelled prior to then, some fairly intensive operations in the yard would be possible. That includes the interesting period when Classes 24, 25 and 26 were seen daily at the station

The east side of the site, the area fenced off on the left was previously railway land.

Turning back the clock, the later steam period years would certainly offer more operating potential, but locomotives would be limited, principally to the LMS Black Fives that made the line their very own up until 1962. However, even then pre-grouping stock could still appear from time to time, and ancient Highland locomotives, whilst the station pilot would frequently be a Caledonian 0-4-4T. Turning the clock back even further, a good few Highland Railway locomotive kits are available, certainly in 4mm scale and in real life, the magnificent green livery of the Highland stock would have been quite impressive during the period leading up to the Great War. That is not to say the beautiful red of the LMS livery would have been diminished by the 1920s and ‘30s. The steam period was certainly an evocative era when we discuss Scottish railways.

Today, it is the omnipresent Class 158 DMUs, which ply between Inverness and Kyle, although during the period I was making some observations, I noted one working was actually between Aberdeen and Kyle. As the Class 170s reach Inverness and Aberdeen, perhaps it is only a matter of time before that class of DMU is found at this charming outpost. As I mentioned, most of the sidings have been rationalised over the years, but a single siding was relaid for off-loading freight, most of it carried in containers I believe. A concrete hard standing area has been put down and the siding is now completely fenced off from the rest of the station site. This area is actually where the steam and early diesel era hard standing was located, so little has really changed.

Looking towards the station throat, access to the shed was just beyond the bridge.

On that recent visit it was interesting to note that the yard area and the land around the station seemed to be taken over with much nautical clutter as well as examples of permanent way materials. Indeed, a smallish fishing boat was out of the water close to the tracks, and I do not mean a rowing boat! Also close to the station was a helicopter pad, which is no doubt used for air-sea rescues and the like. The noise created by the helicopter taking off was tremendous, far louder than a Sulzer Class 26, but it added to the seafaring image of the whole site.

I have split the track plans for this project into two distinct designs. We have the current rationalised track plan as the main project. This plan, whilst not uninteresting would perhaps be suitable for as a starter project by someone interested in the current scene, although modeller's licence would enable a more varied amount of workings. Of course this classic station was well photographed in the steam days and if you wanted to transpose it back to then it would be the simple matter of adding in the missing tracks to my plan. During the Highland Railway period, there were further cross-sidings, feeding the whole site through small wagon turntables: really quite an elaborate affair.

The second, smaller plan is related to Kyle of Lochalsh's diminutive locomotive depot, which was reached just beyond the throat of the station. I include this design because of my interest in small Scottish locomotive depots. There is a sturdy stone built two road locomotive shed and an excellent over-bridge to once again disguise the exit to the station or hidden sidings. The plan is for adaptation, rather than for recreating that at Kyle itself and the slightly elaborate throat to the depot could be altered to avoid the single slip, and the turntable, coaling and watering facilities could be omitted if operating the layout, as I suggest, with diesel locomotives. A re-fuelling facility may be needed instead on a diesel depot, although it could be assumed fuel oil was pumped out of barrels, as in an emergency. Slightly larger than my own *Lochty Road* layout, it is nevertheless a small compact depot and I feel it could be used in 7mm scale (below), with three or four highly detailed diesel locomotives all complete with DCC effects, especially sound and lights and even exhaust smoke. The prices of 7mm diesel locomotives are not low, but this would probably make a 'stand-alone' 7mm project, easily fitted in a reasonable space. I would suggest about 9' with everything, including some hidden run-offs, built on two sturdy baseboards and complete with its own lighting facia for exhibition use. I do however, accept no responsibility for what the exhibitors either side of such a project would say about the smell and the noise: I will leave that to your imagination!

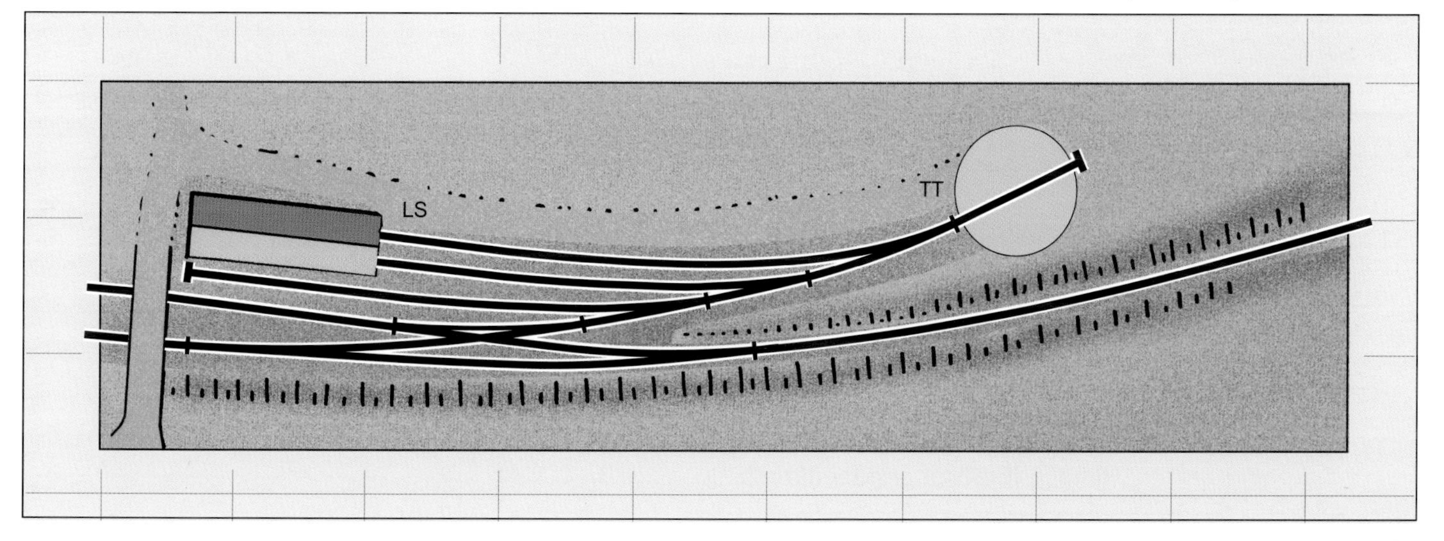

Craigellachie

A rural junction in Malt Whisky country

The Spey, one of Scotland's greatest rivers, is over a hundred miles in length. Its source is high in the Monadhliath mountain range, to the west of Aviemore, from where it flows north eastwards to its mouth on the Moray Firth. It traverses some of the most breathtaking scenery in central Scotland, winding its way from rugged uplands, through sparsely populated countryside to gentle arable lowlands. Frequently the river is hidden away from the main road with the result that much of its natural beauty is lost to the eye. However, much of its beauty could once be seen from the windows of a railway carriage as, until October 1965, it was possible to travel by train from Boat of Garten to Craigellachie along a route which saw the river and railway wending inseparably through the landscape. These two stations earmarked the start and finish of what became known universally as the Speyside line. Other routes connected with both stations: one from Aviemore on the Highland main line to the southern end at Boat of Garten; and two from both Elgin and Keith on the Inverness – Aberdeen route, to the northern end at Craigellachie. Altogether, they formed a distinctive network of rural lines which had operated in this region of north east Scotland for over one hundred years or so.

Although the Great North of Scotland Railway Company would eventually own and run these lines, the early railways were actually quite local concerns and built to provide outlets to the wider world for people and goods. Craigellachie was first connected to the railway network from Keith via Dufftown in 1863. At the same time, a line came into the

Left: the main box at Craigellachie, situated on the north side of the station. It is classic GNoSR design and just to the front of it, to the right of the photograph, the automatic token apparatus is visible. (Photo: J J Davies)

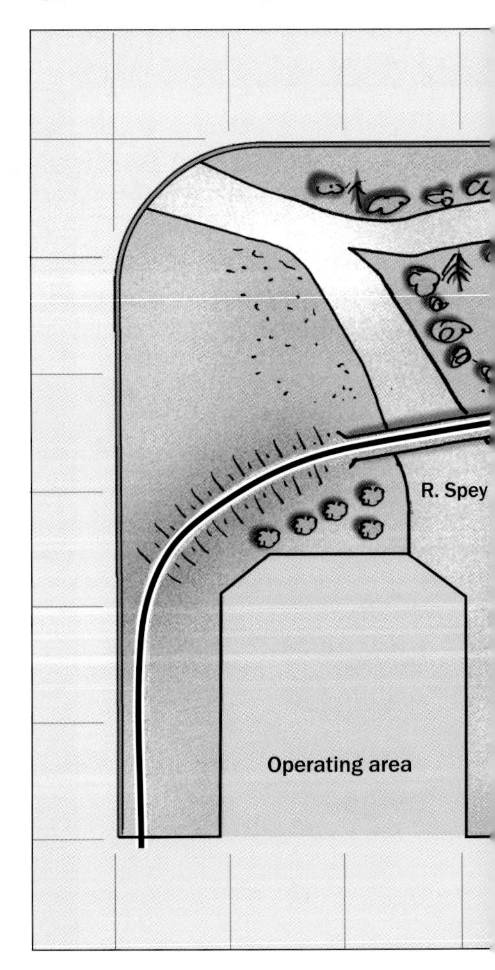

Craigellachie at a glance

Design Scale:	4mm.
Location:	Spey Valley, north east Scotland.
Period:	Post nationalisation to 1970.
Size of Layout:	16ft x 5ft plus room for fiddle yards: by adding another 5ft for these the layout could be squeezed into a 16ft x 10ft garden shed.
Motive Power:	GNoSR 4-4-0s CR 0-6-0, BR 2MT & 4MT Diesel Classes; 21, 24, 25, 26, plus railbuses.
Typical Traffic:	Passenger, general freight, plus whisky and timber, fertiliser and feedstock.

town from the north from Elgin via Rothes. Craigellachie was next linked to Nethy Bridge south westwards along the Spey valley. That also occurred in 1863, but by 1866, the route was finished further west to join the Highland Railway at Boat of Garten.

Eventually, the GNoSR was taken over by the LNER, along with the NBR in the Grouping of 1923, but the pattern of operation along the Speyside line remained much as it had been since the railway had been completed: those beautiful GNoSR 4-4-0 locomotives continued, with

Right: illustrating just why the Speyside line was not commercially viable - an unidentified Class 26 and an ex-LMS brake 3rd form a modeller's sized train for Aviemore in 1965. (Photo: Roy M. Crombie)

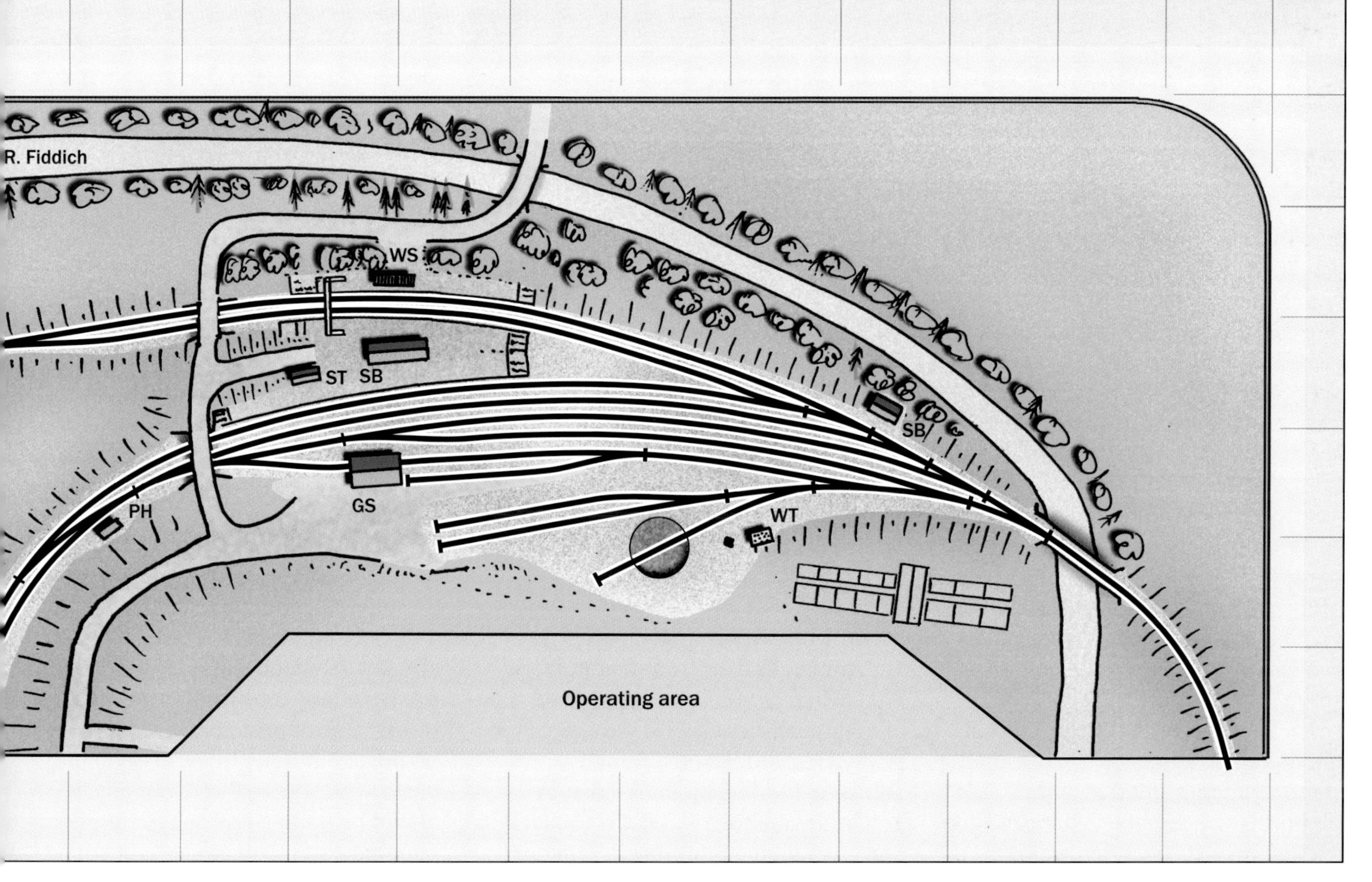

their four and six-wheeled coaches, to trundle slowly alongside the banks of the Spey. During the later LNER period, other locomotives were found on the line, such as the ex-Caledonian types illustrated opposite, along with bogie coaching stock.

Since the early days, Craigellachie had been a sprawling country junction station. It changed little over the years, occupying land surrounded on two sides by rivers; the Spey and its tributary the Fiddich. From the early days of the railway, a triangular platform existed with one platform (3) serving the Boat of Garten services, and the other platform (2) tending to the needs of the Elgin – Lossiemouth trains. A further platform (1) was reached via a footbridge from platform 2, and this served the Dufftown and Keith section. Run round loops were provided, not only for passenger trains but also for freight trains, which were naturally marshalled at Craigellachie. A small goods yard, which included a typical GNoSR wooden goods shed, stood opposite the Boat of Garten platform.

The Boat of Garten and Elgin/Keith tracks formed quite an elaborate junction with a turntable placed nearby. The Speyside route was operated as a separate branch line, with usually three services each way, plus additional trains on Saturdays. The Elgin – Dufftown – Keith section was linked to Lossiemouth services, which in turn connected in with main line services on the Inverness – Aberdeen route.

The line to Rothes and Elgin crossed the River Spey on a substantial enclosed steel girder bridge to the north of the junction. The south bound line, to Dufftown and Keith, also had to make a river crossing which was just to the south of the station. The line to Boat of Garten, accompanied by a long headshunt, on the other hand took a sharp left hand turn to follow the south bank of the River Spey. From photographic evidence, a stone built station building stood between platforms two and three since the line opened, whilst a wooden waiting room stood on platform 1. Loops served the goods shed and there were two further sidings into the goods yard. It was on the approach to the goods yard that the turntable siding was situated. Close by were two further loops next to the run round loop of platform 3. It would have been these tracks that connecting freight stock would have waited upon before continuing their journey along the Speyside line. The station was not very close to the town centre, but the station site was linked with roads and plate girder road bridges. The main signal box stood close to the actual junction itself.

From time to time, Craigellachie would have been a hive of activity, a typical country junction with an interesting selection of passenger and freight trains. Freight traffic would have included vans and wagons for the numerous whisky distilleries situated along the route. Timber would have been a further important source of traffic. Most of the passenger services would have consisted on an assortment of non-corridor coaches. Examples of actual GNoSR rolling stock would have still seen use for many years as well as ex LMS and LNER coaching stock. As the BR Mk1 coaches entered service on main lines, older LMS and LNER corridor stock would have found its way onto Craigellachie services.

The sort of locomotives found on the line in steam days included the elegant GNoSR 4-4-0s (D40 and D41), these remained on the line until the end of steam along with some elderly ex-LNER K2s allocated to Keith shed. Some BR Standard Class 2 and Class 4 2-6-0s also found their way along the routes and freight services ended up in the hands of some ancient CR 0-6-0s. Steam services more or less ended in June 1960 when Keith shed closed, diesel traction took over from that point. Interested modellers of the period will find green liveried EE Class 20s, NB Class 21s and Sulzer Class 26s utilising the line up until closure.

By November 1958 the passenger services on the Speyside line in particular were in the hands of the diminutive four-wheeled railbuses. Examples from Bristol, Park Royal and Wickham builds were all tried out, with varying degrees of success. Ironically, timings along the Speyside line actually improved at this point!

From a modelling point of view, the old Airfix (now Dapol) Park Royal railbus is an ideal candidate for use on such a layout, and a sample number for such a unit is SC79970. Other DMU classes were utilised on passenger services from time to time, including Cravens Class 105 types, usually two-car sets were sufficient for the meagre passenger traffic.

Closure of these branch lines was quite prolonged in some respects. The passenger services between Craigellachie and Boat of Garten ended in October 1965. Freight services survived on the full route until November 1968, though the section to Aberlour lingered until November 1971. The Elgin to Keith route lost its passenger services in May 1968, with freight between Elgin and Craigellachie finishing six months later. The section between Craigellachie and Dufftown finally closed along with the Aberlour section in November 1971, Dufftown, becoming a freight terminus for grain and coal until the 1980s.

To operate Craigellachie with authentic steam traction, modellers will have to resort to white-metal or etched brass kits. The D41 and K2 were both originally manufactured by Nu-Cast and may still be available. I believe an etched brass or white-metal CR Jumbo is also still available too. Strangely enough, the steam stock is also available in 7mm scale as etched kits. Suitable coaching stock and freight stock is also readily available in both scales.

Modelling Craigellachie is therefore a distinct possibility and in fact, has already been done so in 4mm scale by my friends at the Moray Model Railway Group and is regularly seen on the exhibition circuit in Scotland, but beware a model of Craigellachie would be quite a size as the suggested plan indicates. Nevertheless it would

Locomotive Interlude

All the Scottish pre-grouping railway companies built and operated some splendid locomotives, but some of the most enduring types that survived well into British Railways days were of Caledonian Railway parentage. Notably the McIntosh 0-4-4T illustrated below and fully restored in CR livery. Frequently amongst the layout descriptions throughout this book, you will come across references to this type which could be found on many a branch line after the grouping. Similarly, the 'Jumbo' 0-6-0 freight class, illustrated left in full CR blue, followed a similar career across Scotland. Much later, preserved No. 828 is seen here at Boat of Garten in 1994. (Photographs: Frank Hornby and SRPS)

make a very rewarding project for an individual modeller in a suitable home location; a 16' x 12' garden shed or garage would just about do in 4mm scale, though my plan would also be workable with a bit of pruning.

Happily a flavour of travel in this locality can still be experienced. Although a Highland Railway station, it is still possible to ride behind preserved steam and diesel at Boat of Garten on Strathspey Railway, and hopefully, services will soon reach as far as Grantown (HR) in the not too distant future. Equally, preserved rolling stock can be seen on the Keith and Dufftown Railway too. In fact, a holiday in the area is well worth the effort in order to soak up the atmosphere of the old Highland and Great North of Scotland companies.

Bridge of Gairn

A supposed extension of the Royal Deeside route

Plans to serve the River Dee valley with a railway were first mooted in 1845 and before too long a route was proposed to link Aberdeen with Banchory, a distance of about sixteen miles. The railway was authorised a year later, but a number of issues ensured the venture was delayed. This was mainly due to other lines being constructed in the neighbourhood, as well as the usual problem of money being in short supply. As a result, other schemes received priority. It was to be 1852 before a start was made although the first services were operating by September 1853. Plans to extend the line, first of all, to Alford were proposed, but after conflict with the fledgling Great North of Scotland railway company, it was decided to attempt an extension to Aboyne, further up Deeside. In any case, many of these rural lines had to follow the topography of the land and Alford would eventually receive its own branch line.

One of the main reasons for building a railway in Deeside was linked to Royal patronage. The Prince Consort had leased the Balmoral Estate in 1848 and thus the first of many visits to the area took place. Eventually, the Balmoral estate was purchased by the Royal family and it subsequently passed to Queen Victoria. It has remained within the Royal family ever since, becoming a favourite retreat for the late Queen Mother. The extension to Aboyne was authorised in 1857 although in order to secure a better site for Aboyne station, the railway was extended past its authorised finishing point. The line opened in 1859 but the final section was not fully authorised until 1862.

Not Royal Deeside, but Strathyre on the Caledonian in 1958. The ornamental bird bath in the forecourt gives some idea of the sort of feature intended for this plan.

The next extension was proposed to go from Aboyne to Braemar, much further up the Dee Valley and it would appear alarm bells started to ring in the Highland Railway camp. However, it could also be said that perhaps Queen Victoria, who was quite happy to travel by train, was 'not amused' at the thought of roaring steam engines coming rather close to her Balmoral retreat. After looking at a map, you would also wonder why the Highland Railway seemed upset. West of Braemar is basically mountainous and miles from their main route. In any case, it was decided to build the new section only as far as Bridge of Gairn. The main terminus was to be constructed at

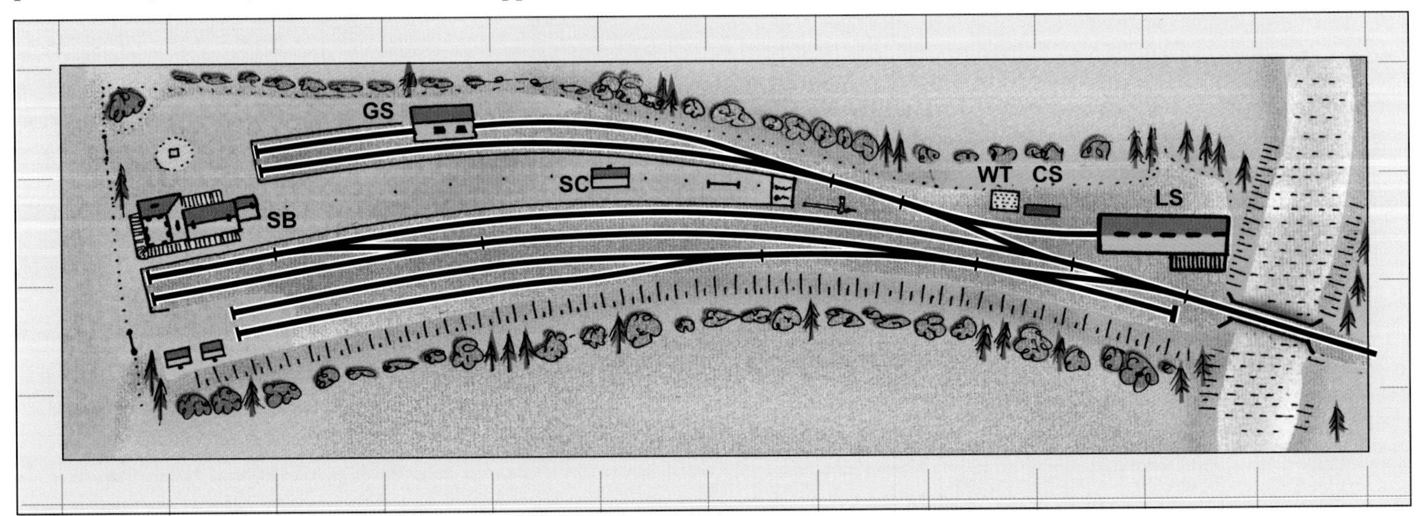

Ballater, about one and a half miles east of Bridge of Gairn. The section between Ballater and Bridge of Gairn was to be freight only. In this form, the railway was authorised in 1865 although provision was made for extensions further west to only go ahead utilising special legislation.

Apparently, by 1866 the line was complete to Ballater, with some work having been carried out to Water of Gairn. In 1868, a contractor was authorised to complete the railway to Bridge of Gairn, from where he proposed a 'tramway' for the twelve miles further west to Braemar. This was in order to transport timber from the area. Consequently, the line was constructed from Ballater, through a cutting and along the banks of the Dee to the Water of Gairn. Bridge abutments were built here in order for the railway to cross the river and terminate at Bridge of Gairn station. At this point the story comes to a dramatic end. The bridge across the river was never built and the rails already laid were lifted. The fact that Queen Victoria eventually purchased much of the forested land could have had a bearing on the extension to Braemar and no doubt she did want the Balmoral estate to remain isolated as such.

It has however, allowed a superb 'just supposing' scheme to be planned to the terminus at Bridge of Gairn, a delightful Scottish name if ever there was one, and the eventual BR Scottish Region blue name-board, would have looked superb. I have terminated the line just across the Water of Gairn, and included a small engine shed by the river itself. Certainly during British Railways days in the 1950s and '60s, the first trains of the day set off to Aberdeen from Deeside, so at least one locomotive would have been stationed there. A modest two-road goods yard includes a typical GNoSR timber goods shed and I have placed the signal cabin on the platform. A pair of carriage sidings is included for when the Royal train brought its visitors to Balmoral, and I have indicated a fine stone station building, with perhaps a turret or two and certainly expansive canopies, in order to keep the royal parties dry. In the station forecourt a clock tower or floral display would not be out of place either.

The operation of such a terminus could be interesting, with on occasions quite long trains of corridor stock. During the steam period, the exquisite GNoSR 4-4-0 locomotives would have been on many of the local services although from the early 1950s some D34 'Glen' 4-4-0s were transferred to Aberdeen, so they would have been seen on the branch. Modellers in 4mm and 7mm scale can obtain kits for such locomotives. Standard Class 4MT tank locomotives were also found on the branch passenger services with the D40/D41 4-4-0s operating freight. A further interesting fact shows that the passenger services on the Deeside Branch ceased in February 1966 with freight services finishing five months later. That brings us neatly into the early diesel period. The line remained open for freight as far as Culter until January 1967.

My timetables for the early 1960s show that diesel services were introduced on the branch and by 1962 some of the services were being operated with the Battery operated railcars Sc79998 and Sc79999. These two units were experimental and resembled Derby Lightweight units. They were withdrawn about the same time passenger services ceased on the Aberdeen - Ballater service, but from all accounts,they were frequently out of service and had to be replaced with normal diesel operation. That would indicate the use of Class 24, 25 and 26 locomotives and perhaps the same locomotive types would have been used on freight services too. The line, despite its Royal patronage, has not had the coverage other Scottish lines have received, and thus photographs of the line seem scarce.

The Deeside line was always a picturesque line and it is welcome news that part of the route is preserved at Crathes (Royal Deeside Railway), where the two-car battery unit is to be found. Parts of the route can still be followed, as with many disused railway lines in Scotland. The Royal family still travel up to Balmoral for holidays and quite frequently attend the Highland Games within the vicinity. It is just a great pity they can no longer travel by train. The Ballater branch line, and therefore our imaginary extension, closed perhaps a little too early in the 1960s before the preservation movement had a chance to check out its potential. It would have made an ideal Scottish preserved railway, having its starting base in Aberdeen or nearby. I suppose now, a model of the line will just have to suffice.

Bridge of Gairn at a glance

Design Scale:	**4mm.**
Location:	**River Dee valley between Ballater and Crathie.**
Period:	**Pre-grouping through to 1970s to suit.**
Size of Layout:	**12ft x 3ft 3ins plus space for fiddle yard.**
Motive Power:	**Dependent on period - see text.**
Typical Traffic:	**Branch passenger including Royal patronage, general merchandise, coal, agricultural products, timber, quarried stone, livestock.**

Alyth

A branch terminus off the Caley's Strathmore route

The Caledonian Railway's main line to the north ran inland through Strathmore in Perthshire on its onward route to the coast at Stonehaven and eventually Aberdeen. Anglo-Scottish traffic was very lucrative and both the Caley and the North British vied for it. Within the Tayside area, Kinnaber Junction was the meeting point of the CR and NBR routes and the famed 'Race to the North' services effectively ended here. In the end, the former North British route held sway between Perth, Dundee and Arbroath, and still survives to this day. Nevertheless, the Caledonian line between Perth, Coupar Angus, Alyth Junction and Forfar was an equally important route in its day. Expresses between Glasgow and Aberdeen took as little as three and a half hours to cover the route, eventually it was the realm of Black Fives, and for a short period before the route closed to passenger services, the swan song of the LNER A4 locomotives.

It is only by looking at old railway maps, that it is possible to see that the Caledonian were involved in a series of short branch lines heading northwards from the Strathmore route. Most of them survived into the 1960s, certainly for freight, though they invariably lost their passenger services in the 1950s. Branches were built to Blairgowrie, Alyth, Kirriemuir, and a through route constructed between Forfar and Brechin. This was closed at the Brechin end in 1958, but remained open as far as Careston until the mid-1960s. Other branch lines in the vicinity included a short branch to Bankfoot, close to Stanley Junction and Perth, and one to Methven off the Strathfillan route to Crieff.

For this scheme, I chose Alyth, for no other reason than it seemed to be an intruiging terminus at the end of a five mile-or-so branch from Alyth Junction. The line opened in 1861. Its operation was closely linked to the Newtyle line, which was in itself, closely linked to Dundee services. From Alyth Junction, the line headed northwards with a station at Meigle and a halt at Jordanstone, which was two miles from the terminus. Between Jordonstone and the terminus was a halt called Golf Club Halt, serving the local links. There had actually been a small goods siding at this site for many years, though it would appear that it was soon abandoned because of lack of use: I can find no reference to the halt in the timetables, or indeed any observation of both stations on assorted maps. Jordonstone is mentioned in a 1950s timetable.

By this time however, there were only two trains each day, and they were linked into Newtyle.

By the following summer, the passenger services were withdrawn from the branch, on 2nd July 1951, to be precise. Freight services, however, lingered on until 1st March 1965.

The countryside served by the branch, is a rich agricultural area, crop growing, cereal and root, as well as cattle rearing being prevalent. There was also further seasonal traffic in such crops as strawberries. The little town of Alyth, sits on the edge of an extensive heather clad moorland, which stretches northwards all the way to Braemar and Deeside.

The station was situated at the southern edge of the town and occupied a triangular site. As the plan shows, the passenger platform was very close to the goods shed, and a loading bank siding was next to the siding running into the goods shed, which was built of local stone. Behind

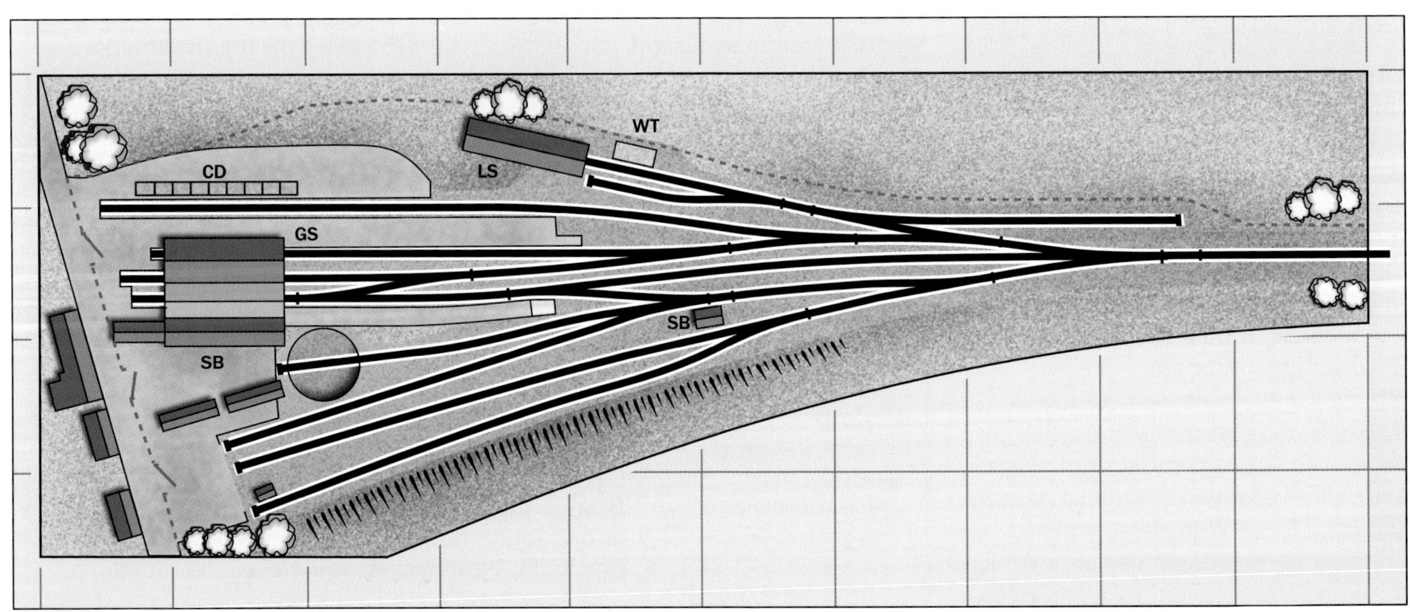

this tall loading bank, which was much higher than the average level of standard van floors, was an additional goods siding, serving some cattle pens. A crossover allowed the passenger locomotive to run round its train but this meant crossing over to the very short siding leading into the goods shed. In earlier days, rolling stock would therefore have had to be carefully placed around the station during shunting, although with only two passenger trains a day, perhaps this might not have been too great a problem. I will mention more of this particular problem later, because of changes made to the track layout at the turn of the twentieth century.

A locomotive shed and turntable eventually featured at the site. The turntable was apparently 42ft in diameter. The locomotive shed at Alyth closed in 1942, no doubt due to war-time economies, being a sub-shed of Dundee, but it was still found to be in use up until 1950. It is this aspect of the station plan, which threw up the most difficulties. Early O.S. plans show the engine shed and turntable occupying space to the south of the platform. However, I have found the Caley decided to build a new brick locomotive shed in the very early 1920s, because the original shed had burnt down in 1916. This new shed was located on a different site, to the north of the platforms, and consisted of a single track shed, along with a short coal siding, from which coal could be loaded directly from wagons onto the locomotives. A headshunt was also incorporated in the scheme.

Earlier, in 1905 a new loop was put in at the end of the platform, from which the turntable siding and original goods yard sidings evolve. During the same period, the crossover was added between the platform and the goods shed siding. This then allowed the passenger locomotive to run-round its coaches. Previously, a fair amount of tow-rope shunting had taken place. I must be honest and say much of the above information was eventually sorted out from old photographs I had seen. A third edition O.S. map (1922) does not apparently exist of Alyth, so most of the published track plans one finds regarding the station, are straight copies of what appeared there pre-1922. Therefore, I am assuming the turntable remained where it was, and was always of a 42ft diameter type, and the set of goods yard sidings also remained much the same. The new locomotive shed could house two CR tank locomotives and was of single track construction. The small signal box closed in 1935, no doubt due to financial economies, as well as staffing issues. Consequently, most of the turnouts seem to be operated with individual hand levers.

An overall roof extended from the station building across to the goods shed but had gone certainly by the 1950s. Close to the new locomotive shed was a small bothy for the locomotive crews, and on top of the bothy was a substantial water tank. The line had always been operated with the traditional Caledonian 0-4-4T locomotives, certainly up until the end of passenger operations in 1951. Just for the record, the previous year had seen 55194 operating the passenger services. Small CR 0-6-0 tender locomotives of equal vintage, would have operated the freight workings. I have however, seen a photograph of an ex-NBR C16 locomotive on shed in 1950 (67483), probably from Dundee Shed. It is possible other classes of locomotive, including ex-NBR 0-6-0 types would have made their way onto the branch, certainly after nationalisation. However, for those modellers who prefer the smaller pre-grouping items of motive power, Alyth remained a Caley outpost for many a year, despite the centre of power turning to Derby after the Grouping. Passenger trains invariably consisted of just an LMS brake third non-corridor vehicle, that is, once the Caledonian coaches had been withdrawn.

So, an archetypal branch line terminus suited to steam operation. It changed a little over the years with the attempt to ease the operations by changing the track plan slightly. Obviously, to model the branch during the early Caledonian period, the original track plan would need to be adhered to, my plan will suit devotees of the LMS or BR periods. Little is heard about these small branch lines in the Strathmore region, yet I find many of their histories intriguing and the research captivating. If you are ever want to find out more about these obscure railways of Scotland, simply put the name of your interested project into an Internet search engine on a computer: I think you could well be pleasantly surprised, as there are a lot of folk out there providing useful and accessible information for us railway modellers.

Alyth at a glance

Design Scale:	**4mm.**
Location:	**Strathmore, Perthshire.**
Period:	**1930s - 1950s.**
Size of Layout:	**10ft x 3ft 6ins max., plus space for fiddle yard.**
Motive Power:	**Mainly ex-Caledonian types until after Nationalisation when NB types could be seen.**
Typical Traffic:	**Passenger, coal, general merchandise, livestock, agricultural produce.**

Glenfinnan

The best known station on the Mallaig extension

The Mallaig Extension opened on the 1st April 1901 linking Fort William with the Atlantic Coast. From the start, fish had been the main reason for linking Mallaig to the railway network, although it must be remembered, towards the end of the nineteenth century, there had been concerns in Parliament about the plight of the crofters and islanders in the Highlands. The Mallaig link was set up to aid the Western Islanders with an additional route to Glasgow and the lowlands. The Oban and Kyle of Lochalsh routes were already established by this time. The stations along the Mallaig route were never going to be busy with passengers, but they have served their local communities for over a hundred years, and long may they continue to do so.

Glenfinnan is a location of great historical interest; Bonnie Prince Charlie allegedly unfurled his Standard there in 1745, prior to the uprising that culminated in the famous battle on Drumossie moor at Culloden. A tall monument to recognise the great event stands to this day and can be glimpsed from the train as it crosses the Finnan Valley on a magnificent viaduct built on a 12 chain radius curve. This beautifully formed concrete structure stands 100ft above the valley floor, the graceful piers, encompassing 21 semi-circular arches, each with a span of 50ft. The viaduct is 1248ft in length and impressive rocky cuttings are to be found at either end. Close to the viaduct is Glenfinnan station, a typical example of a Mallaig extension passing loop station. Fortunately, most of the trackwork is still in-situ along with the original buildings. As a result, we have been able to provide this project with scale drawings and a host of photographs, to enable an accurate model to be constructed. I believe it could be built either in 2mm, 4mm and even 7mm scale, if suitable space were available. Locomotives and rolling stock are available in all three scales.

In June 1983 37178 drifts away from Glenfinnan with the mid morning service for Mallaig. The EE Type 3 is surely over-powered for this two coach train, but isn't it just a superb prototype for the space starved modeller?

The main passing loop is situated on a generous curve, and unlike stations on the 'main line', with their wide island platforms, Glenfinnan follows true Mallaig Extension practice in having two concrete platforms opposite each other. Surprisingly, there are no footbridges on the line. Passengers are required to use the barrow style crossings at the ends of the platform. A good old-fashioned example of Scottish common sense! If there have been any accidents over the years, nobody seems to have mentioned it! A small wooden waiting

Glenfinnan at a glance

Design Scale:	**4mm (EM or P4) but adaptable for all others.**
Location:	**The Mallaig extension at the head of Loch Sheil.**
Period:	**Pre-grouping through to present day to suit.**
Size of Layout:	**Visible: 12ft 6ins x 5ft, though could easily be made smaller if using proprietary track.**
Motive Power:	**Pre-grouping to BR: D34 Glen 4-4-0s, J35, J36 0-6-0s, K1, K2, K4 2-6-0s. Diesel Classes; 27, 29 37, occasional 20, 24 and 25.**
Typical Traffic:	**Branch passenger, general merchandise, fish, livestock, coal fuel oil.**

shelter is found on the Fort William bound platform whilst opposite, is the concrete station building itself. Nowadays it houses a museum, but structurally, it is more or less the same as it was on the day it was built.

Close to the station building, still on the platform, is found a small concrete goods shed stands, with doors facing the tracks, and also a further set of doors forming a loading bay, next to the station yard. A further set of doors, are found in one end of the shed, leading to a tiny loading bank. Obviously not a great deal of freight was expected by the NBR. The structures were identical to others found on the line, with another perfect set of them being found at Arisaig. The large, wooden planked signal cabins were also standard for the Mallaig line, and they were in fact, bought 'off the shelf', from a railway signalling company. The example at Glenfinnan still stands although it has been out of use for many years. A small ground frame controls some of the turnouts in the disused yard.

For many years camping coaches were placed in the siding at Glenfinnan, and today, two BR Mk. 1 coaches can be found, one of them serving teas and snacks. The other coach is a sort of 'sleeping coach' for visitors to the area, so the tradition of camping coaches continues. The tracks are still in place at this point, although a small end loading siding, behind the signal cabin, was removed in the 1980s. The old water tank still stands on the hillside behind the Fort William platform. Nowadays, the site is heavily wooded, with a variety of trees to be found. This is in stark contrast to when the line opened, and indeed right up until the 1960s. An old photograph, taken the NBR period, shows the station site devoid of trees, and the rocky outcrop above the Fort William platform showed only a few bushes of gorse and shrubs. Even by the time the diesels commenced operations, the area behind this platform could clearly be seen. The platforms struggle to hold more than

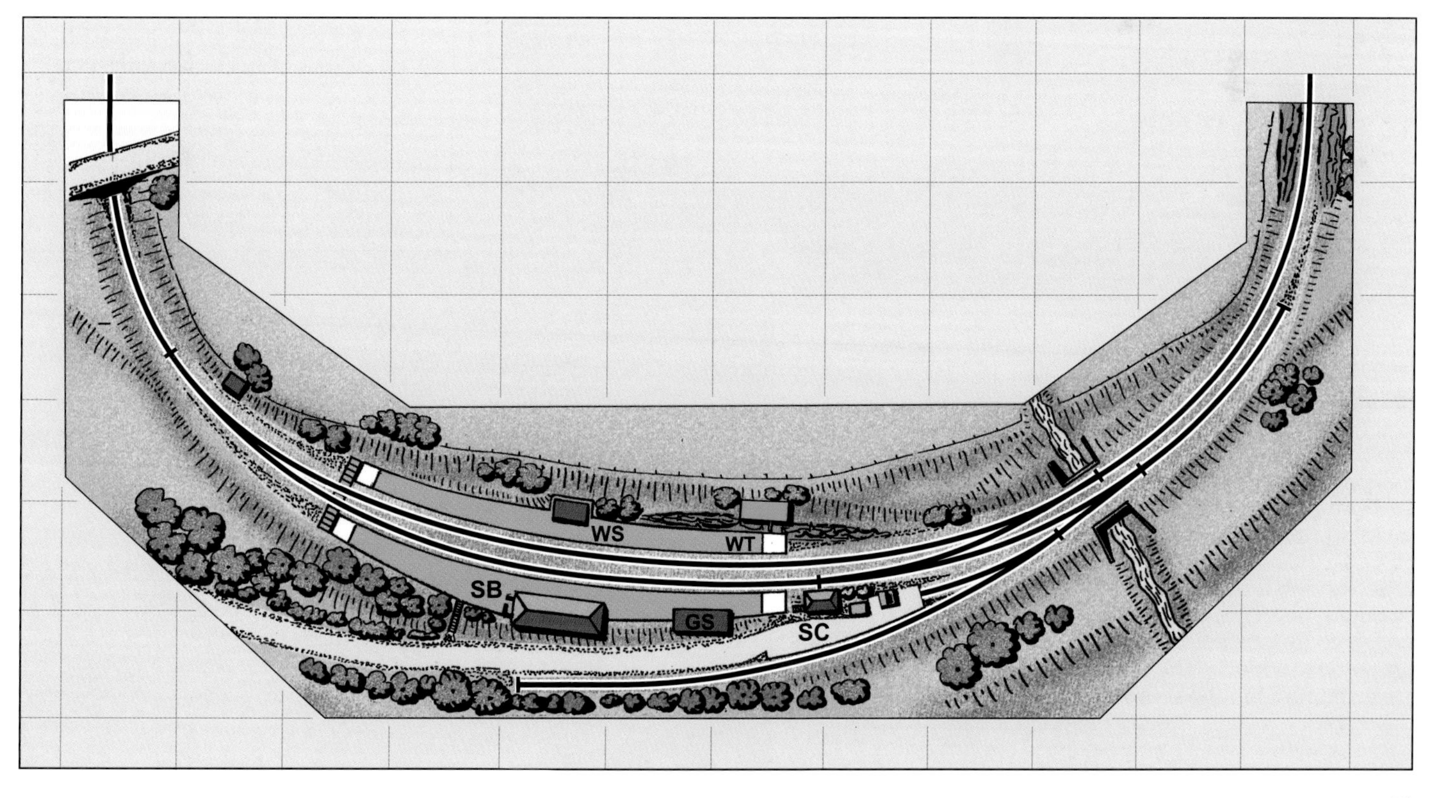

three or four coaches along with their locomotives. An ideal scene for space starved modellers in any scale.

The trackwork should be easily reproduced in either 2mm and 4mm scale, although the plan is drawn so as to make use of handbuilt track with sweeping turnouts. They would need to be laid with care, to allow a smooth transition of stock. Naturally, the main turnouts are sprung-loaded on the passing loop, as is the practice on the line today.

Top: a general view of the station looking towards the Fort William end. This view was taken in 1987 with the Scotrail station signage in place, not present in the colour shots which were taken four years earlier in 1983. The signal box name board has also gone missing within that short period, compare with the view far right on the opposite page. The chalet style main building (above) is in almost the condition it was built 80 or so years earlier, save a coat of paint and some tube lighting under the canopy (top right). On the opposite platform, this timber shelter (near right) was provided for passengers who accessed it via a timber crossing (no footbridge here) at the Mallaig end. The station approach (opposite centre) was on a gentle downward gradient. Goods handling included loading banks and this small concrete store (centre right).

I envisage this plan to be part of a circular track system, with a bank of hidden sidings forming the Mallaig and Fort William sections. The beauty of this station is the fact you can, in 4mm scale at least, operate it as a pure NBR system, utilising the old GEM cast white metal kits. Equally, the layout could be set during the LNER or BR steam periods. Perhaps a good R-T-R K1 or K2 is required, but kits are available. Better still, the layout can be moved into the 1960s or 1970s, with the aid of Heljan or Bachmann products. By setting the layout in the 1980s, the Bachmann or Vi-Trains Class 37s can be utilised, and even the current scene can be operated with Class 156 DMUs. As a bonus, the steam summer specials operated along the line from the 1980s onwards, allowing the use of B1s and Black Fives. Quite a wide choice, I'm sure you will agree.

I should really add, that I have 'doodled' with this plan on many an occasion! The one reproduced here was drawn by Steve Flint many years ago and requires a lot of space in 4mm - 12ft 6ins in length in fact. It was originally drawn with EM or P4 modellers in mind and I'm sure it could be reduced considerably if using OO gauge proprietary trackwork, such that it should fit in a small spare bedroom quite comfortably, or as a stand-alone layout for the exhibition circuit.

What are we waiting for... get out the track planning templates now!

Inveraray

A destination too far

By the late nineteenth century, Inveraray, the county town of Argyllshire was not of any strategic importance regarding the expansion of the railway network in Scotland. It had, however, been the centre of attention from the very early days of the Callander and Oban Railway and that company had made a sort of promise to link its railway by means of a branch line from Dalmally. It must be noted that the C & O promised other similar routes to other settlements, but by the mid 1890s, none had come to fruition. By then, the Caledonian Railway was in control of the route to Oban and the Light Railways Act of 1896, spurred on a sort of mini-railway mania within the Highlands. All sorts of plans were then proposed, passed by the Commissioners, and then never actually completed!

In about 1897, Inveraray attracted the attention of Charles Forman, a partner in the railway contracting firm of Forman and McCall. That company was responsible for building the West Highland Railway, amongst other schemes in Scotland, and routes were frequently called 'contractors railways' because of this. Furthermore, a light railway from Arrochar on the WHR to St Catherines, a sleepy hamlet on the opposite shore of Loch Fyne to Inveraray, was also proposed. Here a ferry would have taken goods and

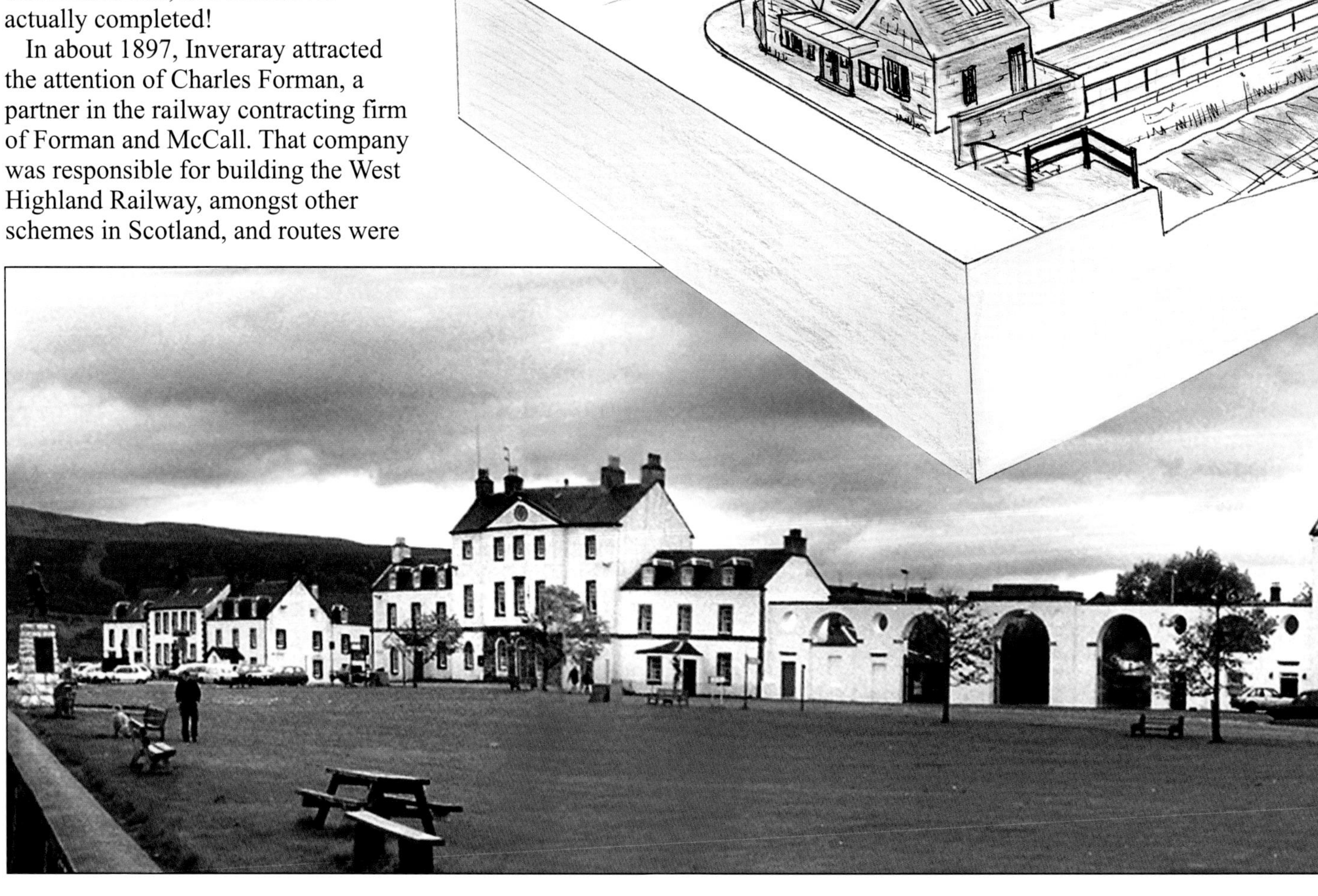

passengers across Loch Fyne to Inveraray itself. So, the Argyllshire county town may just have received two railways on its doorstep - or should that be loch side?

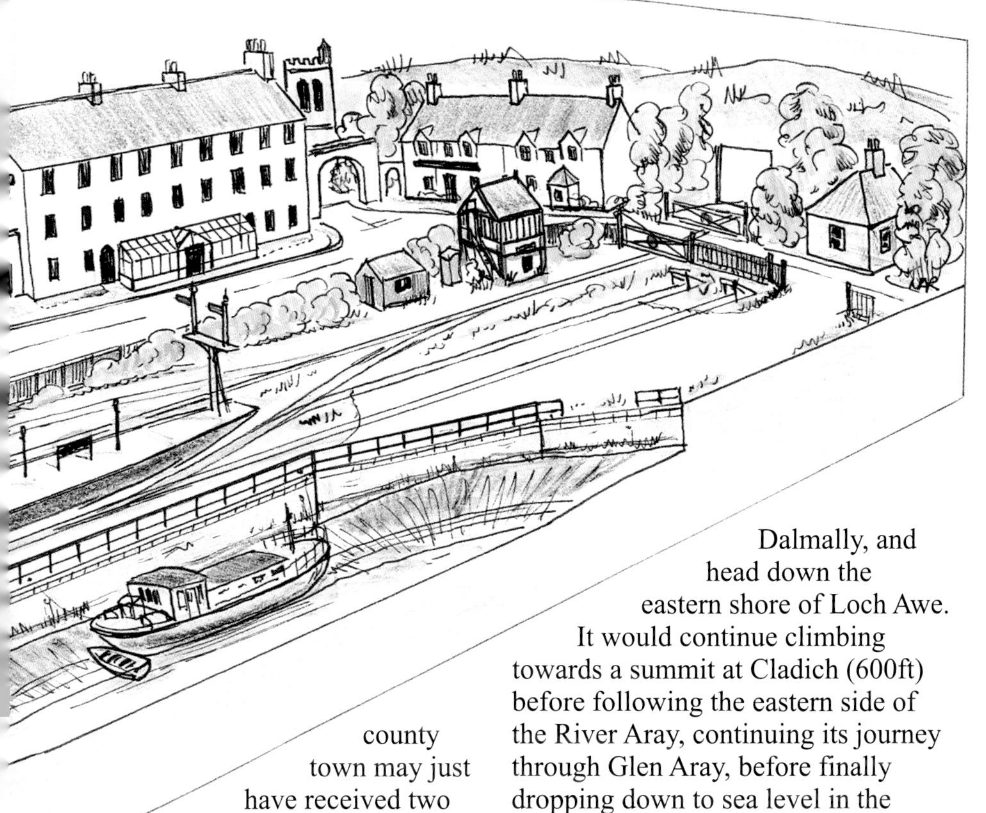

Firstly the Caledonian proposal, this was to branch off the Oban line at Dalmally, and head down the eastern shore of Loch Awe. It would continue climbing towards a summit at Cladich (600ft) before following the eastern side of the River Aray, continuing its journey through Glen Aray, before finally dropping down to sea level in the town. Basically, it is the route of the A819, although that road keeps to the right hand side of the river for the whole of its journey to Inveraray. There was the slight problem of passing underneath the battlements of Inveraray Castle, the seat of the Duke of Argyll. A tunnel was planned at this point despite the expense, but the Duke had no trouble, like many before him, in having the plans thrown out. The line would have been fifteen miles in length from Dalmally. Renditions of both the might-have-been terminus station and the junction at Dalmally have been built in 4mm by Paul Timperley.

On the other side of Loch Fyne, the second proposal, a light railway from Arrochar, was to head through Glen Croe, passing the small settlement of Rest and be Thankful (what a super station name that would have been), then through Glen Kinglas following what is more or less the route of the

If ever there was a natural backscene for a layout, this building frontage, photographed at Inveraray itself in 1983, would surely qualify in first place. The buildings have been incorporated into the layout backdrop in full relief, as illustrated by Neil Ripley's artist's impression of the proposed plan.

A83 today. It would have then dropped down to sea level at Cairndow, and followed the eastern shore of Loch Fyne for about five miles into St Catherines.

I actually researched this route in some detail during the summer of 1999 and I have to say, the gradients would have been horrendous, more so where the line left Arrochar at the head of Loch Long and headed inland through Glen Croe, and on the descent in Glen Kinglas towards Cairndow.

My 7mm layout, exhibited throughout 2000, was naturally called *St Catherines for Loch Fyne*. The fish from Loch Fyne had a lot to do with both proposed lines, and in the end the Light Railway Commissioners opted for the St Catherines route. Its act was passed not long after but the NBR failed to construct the line: Argyll and Inveraray were destined never to have a railway.

Just where all the traffic was to come from is not really known. The landscape, whilst beautiful and wild, had few settlements of note, and even less landowners who could find money to invest in such a scheme. There were also grand ideas to extend the route from Inveraray to Dunoon and other points in Argyllshire, but they all came to naught too: plenty of just supposing schemes of course, ideal for all persuasions of Scottish railway modellers

So to this plan, the basis of which is the Caledonian scheme proposed from Dalmally Junction. It is yet another involving railways and water, as no doubt the station at Inveraray would have been located close to Loch Fyne. Such a plan would not be as grand as say, Oban, after all, twenty years would have passed since Oban station had opened, and railway companies

Inveraray at a glance

Design Scale:	**4mm, though would be manageable in 7mm.**
Location:	**On the shore of Loch Long, Argyllshire.**
Period:	**Pre-grouping through to 1970s to suit.**
Size of Layout:	**8ft x 2ft 6 ins, plus fiddle yard.**
Motive Power:	**ex-Caledonian; McIntosh 0-4-4Ts, Jumbo 0-6-0, diesel Classes; 21, 27.**
Typical Traffic:	**Passenger, general merchandise, fish, fuel oil, coal, agricultural produce.**

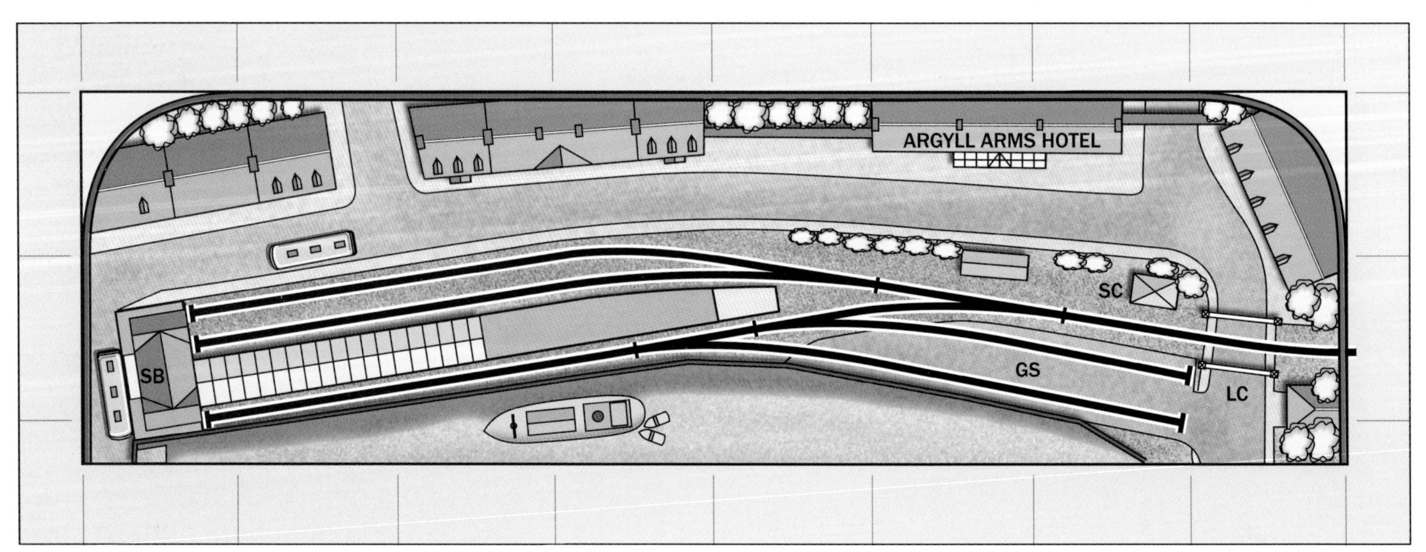

Left: my 7mm layout St Catherines was set on the opposite bank of Loch Fyne and was the 'other' station that could have served Inveraray. The island platform and canopy are the same as those proposed in this plan.

Right: in 1983 tourist coaches park up where the station forecourt would be.

Below: my ex-NBR C15 4-4-2T could well have shunted at Inveraray in BR days.

were no longer spending lots of money on large track layouts and facilities, especially in rural areas. Inveraray station would have been quite modest in comparison, although in reality, it could be made as modest or as grand as you wish: it never existed, so who will be able to say your interpretation is incorrect?

The plan actually follows my original *St Catherines* Plan. I did think a run round to one of the platform faces would make the operation a little easier, but in the end, opted for the services of perhaps a station pilot. Once again, I have assumed freight facilities were off stage, away from the elaborate passenger operations, much like Fort William really. However, a carriage siding is included. A small locomotive shed, with the usual facilities including a small turntable are also imagined to be off stage too. My *St Catherines* layout made great use of the fishing industry, herrings in particular and so somewhere within the confines of the layout, a fish curing and packing factory might be appropriate and

could form a rather nice set of low-relief structures in the background. The waterfront at Inveraray is very attractive as Neil Ripley's exquisite drawing shows. I'm tempted to say, there should also be a plethora of seagulls and guano. Look that one up in a dictionary to get my drift!

Operation of the layout would be pure Caledonian, or at least LMS, if setting the scene after 1923. Even in BR steam days during the early 1950s, the emphasis would have included many CR designs, 0-6-0 Jumbos and similar classes for freight services, as well as some elderly, but quite handsome Pickersgill and McIntosh 4-4-0s. Station pilot duties would necessitate the ubiquitous McIntosh 439 0-4-4T or its LMS cousin - ten further locomotives of this class were built by the LMS in 1925. Passenger rolling stock, even in the 1950s was usually pure LMS and no doubt a small sprinkling of parcels stock would be seen. Fish wagons, again they should be of the LMS variety unless you are modelling the Caledonian Railway period, when they would possibly be in sheeted open wagons like the North British. Parkside-Dundas have a nice 4mm LMS fish van in 4mm scale.

This project is designed for those modellers who are of the Caledonian or Derby persuasion, but once again, you might like to get away with operating the layout with one or two green diesels. On this occasion, modeller's licence assumes that the Inveraray branch would have closed in 1966, along with the Ballachulish branch from Connel Ferry and for inspiration we can draw on numerous photographs and reports of green liveried Type 2 Bo-Bo diesels operating with just one Thompson steel sided non-corridor coach. An integrated service with the Oban line would be essential, though as the line sank deeper into the possibility of closure, it would have become an isolated branch, offering a meagre service into Dalmally. Typical of that period, no doubt the station buildings would have been all spruced up and freshly painted a year or so before closure in 1966. That, in reality was what occurred at a number of stations up and down the glens, just as the end crept silently closer. Locomotives and rolling stock may look distinctly weathered but at least the buildings would have been in pristine condition!

Loch Katrine Pier

A fanciful tourist line in the Trossachs

In my first book, Neil Ripley produced some exquisite watercolour artwork within its pages, and one particular print has encouraged me to design a 'just supposing' layout in the Trossachs. Such a line was considered at the time the Callander and Oban route was moving slowly westwards towards its final destination at Oban. The Caledonian Railway was involved in this venture, started in 1865 as a local concern.

However, the story unfolds in 1870, when news leaked out that the North British were considering building such a line from the old station at Callander. The NBR did not have running powers along the Callander and Oban line, but they did have a special arrangement to send tourist trains to Callander, an arrangement brokered with the CR itself. John Anderson, the erstwhile secretary of the C & O became rather alarmed at the prospect of the NBR entering 'his' territory, so he proposed (more or less by himself) a short branch leaving the main line just west of Callander station. The route was to run for ten miles or so along the north shore of Loch Vennacher, basically where the current A821 runs, to Brig o'Turk: an enchanting name for a station you must agree! It would then continue along the wooded shores of Loch Achray before terminating by the pier at the southernmost tip of Loch Katrine itself. That it would have been a most picturesque branch line, passing through some of the most charming scenery in Scotland, cannot be in doubt.

The Caledonian Railway was a very efficient concern and set to work estimating the possible tourist traffic. Apparently, they were not at all optimistic and despite John Anderson cajoling all and sundry within the district as to the benefits of such a railway to the tourist industry, the venture was quietly forgotten. It would have appeared the NBR were simply testing the water and they too made no further overtures to enter the territory. However, over the ensuring years, the idea of a railway into the heart of the Trossachs was raised occasionally but a line was never built. That is the beauty of 'just supposing' layouts, and of course the name Loch Katrine Pier itself conjures up sights of steam ships alongside steam trains. Although there would have been through tourist services from further afield, a local service between the pier and a bay platform at Callander station would have operated to or three times a day and probably have been in the hands of one of the Caledonian Railway's delightful 0-4-4T classes, complete with a coach or two. The branch would have no doubt been used when the CR, LMS and British Railways each in turn organised their Grand Circular Tours, visiting Callander, Lochearnhead, Crieff, Gleneagles and Stirling all within a day from Glasgow Buchanan Street. That terminus closed in November 1966 by the way.

I imagine Loch Katrine Pier station being located next to the loch itself and surrounded by steep, tree clad hillsides, much as the steamer pier is today in reality. A similarity to other pier stations would be in evidence and I have imagined the station building to be rather elaborate, wooden single story affair, as befitting a Victorian tourist outpost: the Caledonian liked impressive wooden buildings in any case. Alternatively, it could be modelled on Fort Augustus pier station if the fancy takes you, and hopefully, it would have lasted a trifle longer than that station did!

I have assumed one single platform with a simple loop facility, although this could be extended if more space was available in the layout room. A single carriage siding is available, perhaps two would be better. Only the most basic of coal and watering facilities is included as the site is very much restricted by the topography of

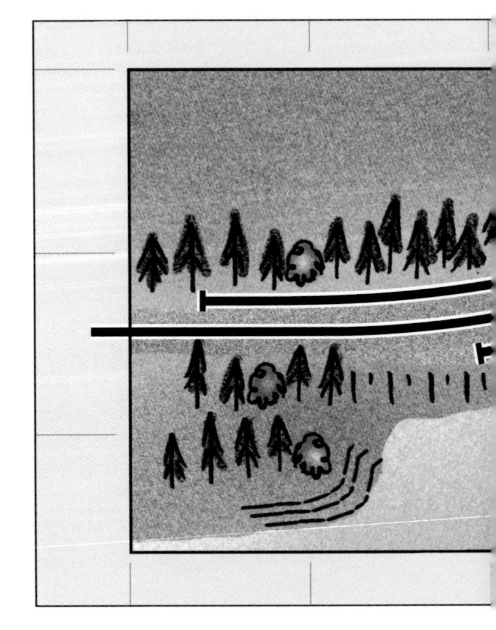

Loch Katrine Pier at a glance

Design Scale:	**4mm, but adaptable to any other.**
Location:	**Beyond Callander at the head of Loch Katrine.**
Period:	**Pre-grouping through to 1970s to suit.**
Size of Layout:	**10ft x 2ft 8ins, though a much thinner board would be desirable to avoid modelling all that open water!**
Motive Power:	**Various dependant on period - see text.**
Typical Traffic:	**Tourist passenger traffic mainly, with perhaps a twice daily branch mixed train in the winter season. Also coal for the Loch Katrine steamer; SS Sir Walter Scott, to its own service pier.**

the surrounding hillsides and precludes a turntable and shed. A basic freight store is included and a short siding for coal for the steamer is installed. I envisage the ex-Caledonian 4-4-0 locomotives, or 4-6-0 types would have been the normal motive power on excursion traffic.

Naturally a small CR timber signal box would have controlled all the movements within the station confines. It is conceivable that a daily freight service would have brought the coal for the steamer plying their way around Loch Katrine, so that would have allowed a modicum of freight stock in the station with all but the coal wagons returning from whence they came.

It is quite a well-known fact that the Stirling to Crianlarich section of the Callander and Oban line lost their services fairly abruptly in 1965 following a landslide in Glen Ogle. The services were under threat anyway, but just supposing the section between Dunblane and Callander had remained and, because of tourism in the Trossachs the little branch to Loch Katrine Pier also remained. The layout could therefore be operated with diesels or, latterly DMUs, even second generation ones. Thus, with digital sound becoming popular, it may soon be possible to recreate the magical Sulzer sound a amongst the Trossach scenery with Classes 24, 25, 26 or 27. As this layout proposal falls into the just supposing category, the imagination can be left to run truly wild, so why not start by checking out Neil Ripley's watercolour on page 68 of my first book and commence with the baseboard construction.

Oh, there is just the slight matter of providing a vintage steamer to fit on the loch. There are a number of ship and boat modelling magazines and specialist model shops to aid you here. Alternatively the model by Artitec could be utilised for placing on that beautiful loch-side location, but don't forget that, the actual steamer, Sir Walter Scott is still in use today; so why not take a pleasant research trip to the pier and gather photographs for a scratchbuilding project that's a little different!

Above: the flavour of Loch Katrine and the Trossachs is captured here with this shot of the pier at Stronachlacher. This is at the far end of the loch with the vintage steamer, Sir Walter Scott, about to embark on its return trip.

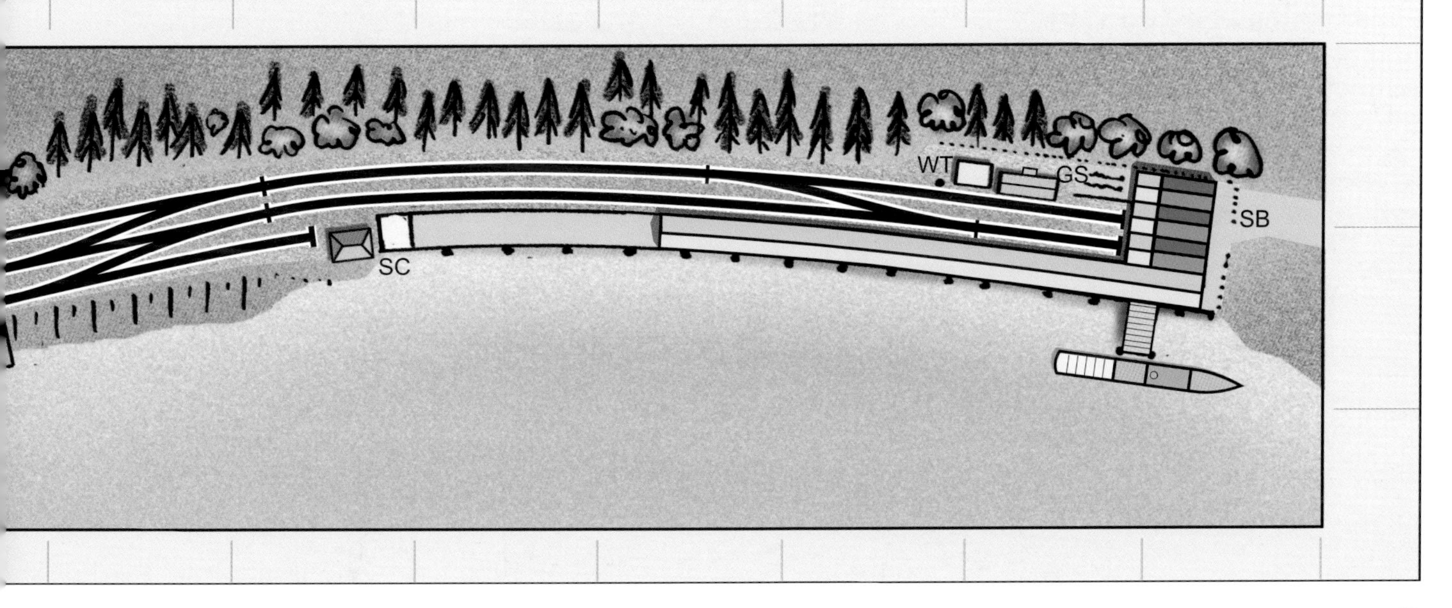

Victoria Park

In the industrial heartlands of Glasgow

Industrial railway sites within Scotland can still be found, although it is fair to say not many are rail connected today. Some newer industries with rail connections exist: they can be found, and frequently, in rural locations, but they tend to have limited siding space, sometimes only one or two tracks. Go back fifty-odd years and the scene was quite different: the life-blood of Scottish railways had always been freight, and many industries, large and small, were connected to the rail network. As a matter of course, from the earliest days of the railways, sidings were laid as and when an industry required some. On the other hand, the railway companies would soon take a siding out of use if the traffic did not warrant it, or it ceased to exist. Even on the rural lines of the NBR in Northumberland, sidings were put into quarries, collieries, lime kilns and the like during the early years but many were out of use and lifted by the time of the grouping in 1923.

Many modellers enjoy building layouts with intensive freight operation. Whether the traffic is coal, minerals, steel or chemicals, industrial layouts require specific rolling stock and often, specific locomotives: many steam locomotives spent their whole working life devoted to hauling a particular commodity and never strayed from one locality or depot.

Likewise, the traditional open style coal or mineral wagon was found in abundant numbers, frequently in colourful pre and post grouping liveries. Even today, much of the colour found on our truncated railway network consists of privately owned locomotives and rolling stock.

Now, one might assume that any model railway constructed with an industrial theme would, by its very nature, be a huge project: a grand expanse of exchange loops perhaps? Not so, since when designing this project, I had *Walker Marine* - an inspirational industrial layout in a small space - and *Clydesdale Iron Foundry* in my thoughts.

Looking through some books of the railways in and around Glasgow, various images set the evocative thoughts flowing. The photographs showed fussy little 'Pugs' (usually ubiquitous 0-4-0 tank locomotives) hauling wagons and bogie-bolster stock, with materials, most usually for the Clyde ship building industry. In fact, further research relating especially to the shipbuilding industry itself, showed much of the Clyde industry relied heavily on rail to supply them with the raw materials. They also relied upon the railways to transport their workers too. Some of the photographs I studied showed vast amounts of sidings covering many acres, but the images that emerged in my mind's eye were on a much smaller and more manageable scale.

In one photograph, I noted a small industrial electric locomotive, shunting some mineral wagons along a typical cobbled street in Govan. Behind all of this was a Glasgow Corporation bus, although it equally may have been a Glasgow tram, and surrounding the whole scene were the tall and foreboding tenement houses, some even complete with small business outlets at street level. It was just this sort of scene I felt could be interesting in model form and somehow, I wanted to see the tracks

Centre: my 7mm layout *Victoria Park* was a portrait of a Glasgow suburban terminus that would have connected to the passenger service featured in this plan. *Victoria Park* appeared in its construction phase in my previous book *Modelling Scotland's Railways.*

Left: the industrial railway scene in the heart of Glasgow was far removed from the romantic ideal of railways elsewhere in Scotland. Victoria Yard aims to replicate that urban industrial hustle and bustle, a taste of which is captured here on this S7 layout - Clydesdale Iron Foundry Co. Ltd.

Photograph: Ian Middleditch

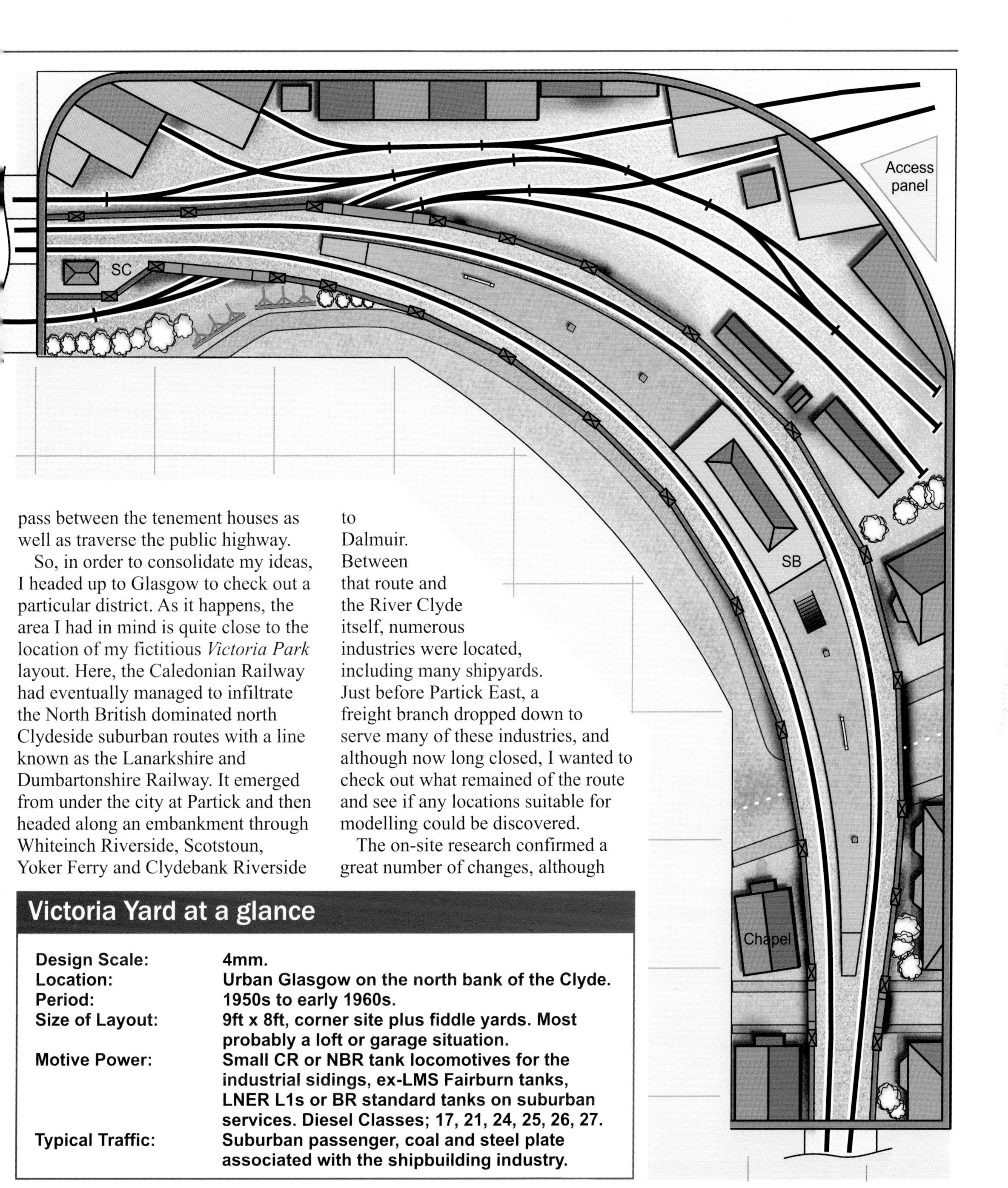

pass between the tenement houses as well as traverse the public highway.

So, in order to consolidate my ideas, I headed up to Glasgow to check out a particular district. As it happens, the area I had in mind is quite close to the location of my fictitious *Victoria Park* layout. Here, the Caledonian Railway had eventually managed to infiltrate the North British dominated north Clydeside suburban routes with a line known as the Lanarkshire and Dumbartonshire Railway. It emerged from under the city at Partick and then headed along an embankment through Whiteinch Riverside, Scotstoun, Yoker Ferry and Clydebank Riverside to Dalmuir. Between that route and the River Clyde itself, numerous industries were located, including many shipyards. Just before Partick East, a freight branch dropped down to serve many of these industries, and although now long closed, I wanted to check out what remained of the route and see if any locations suitable for modelling could be discovered.

The on-site research confirmed a great number of changes, although

Victoria Yard at a glance

Design Scale:	**4mm.**
Location:	**Urban Glasgow on the north bank of the Clyde.**
Period:	**1950s to early 1960s.**
Size of Layout:	**9ft x 8ft, corner site plus fiddle yards. Most probably a loft or garage situation.**
Motive Power:	**Small CR or NBR tank locomotives for the industrial sidings, ex-LMS Fairburn tanks, LNER L1s or BR standard tanks on suburban services. Diesel Classes; 17, 21, 24, 25, 26, 27.**
Typical Traffic:	**Suburban passenger, coal and steel plate associated with the shipbuilding industry.**

there still remained a huge amount of industry. I headed for Clydebank first of all, but much of the land around the riverside area had been cleared. A wander down to Scotstoun and Whiteinch revealed more industrial remnants including a remaining section of the elevated Caledonian line, which is now a pathway and cycle route. I photographed a few of the old bridges, including one over Balmoral Street and proceeded to walk along the old railway line. Imagine my surprise at finding the island platform, which used to belong to Scotstoun station. Better still, the old entrance and booking hall offices were also still in place (below right). A model scenario began to form in my head. Not only that, many of the old tenements were still there, so they were photographed too.

I started to visualise the old Caledonian route running across the whole project allowing a certain amount of passenger operation, although it would be limited to simply stopping and starting at the typical island style platforms. A small freight yard would allow for interchange traffic, which would disappear across cobbled streets and into off-scene industries. The whole scene would include tall tenement buildings with one or two shops underneath, much the same as one sees today as it happens. The whole scene would try and recreate the dourness that seems to be found in the area, although I do admit, it was a rather grey and wet sort of day that greeted me as I wandered around the area, creating some strange looks from the locals as I sketched and photographed the various landmarks.

Once back home, a slight problem occurred each time I sat down to draw out a plan. Different ideas flowed from the pencil and I began to realise that this sort of project could be never ending. To me, it seemed to evolve in many different ways, depending perhaps upon what features a builder may decide eventually to incorporate. I also became acutely aware that the whole project could be possibly placed more or less in any industrial locality within Scotland. The same sort of scene could be found anywhere in Glasgow and possibly in the Leith area of Edinburgh. Another possible location could be Dundee, or indeed one of the many towns within the Central Belt region.

Therefore, my own particular offering should perhaps be suggested as a starting point. Depending upon space and resources, this project typifies the urban approach when modelling such scenes. It need not be too large, and perhaps the actual railway content could be less significant than the scenic or structural content. Although the tenements would really need to be accurately built. It would also be an important requisition to include an element of grime into the scene, so subtle weathering would be important.

Turning to possible motive power for such a layout, the obvious need would be for some small shunting locomotives such as the Caley or North British 'Pug' locomotives. I'm tempted to say even the basic Hornby 0-4-0T locomotives could be deemed suitable. An assortment of traditional wagons and vans, along with some bogie bolster vehicles or plate wagons loaded with sheet metal or girders would not look out of place. Passenger services

Top left: the tenement style buildings which feature in the plan are based loosely on these in Scotstoun.

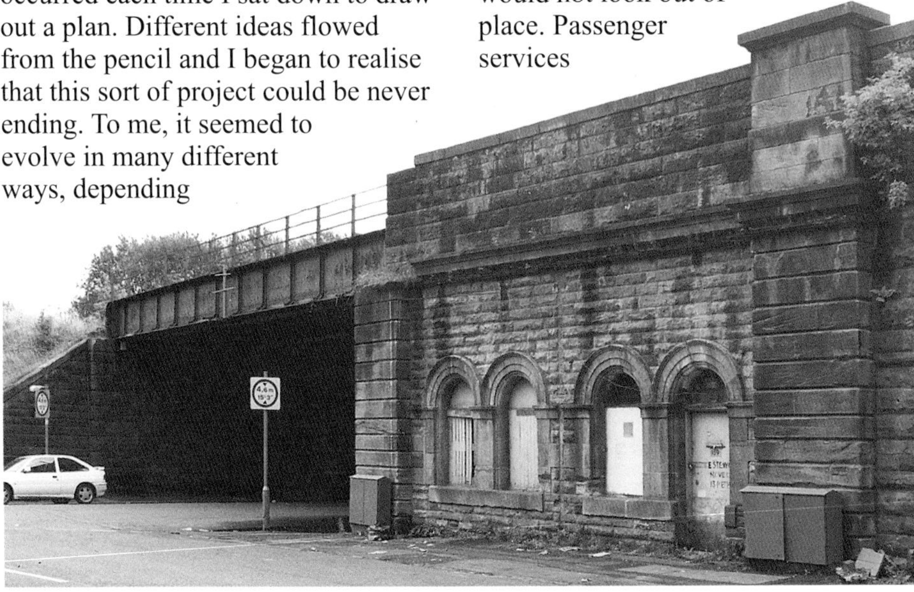

Right: these remains of Scotstoun East Station, with the booking hall on the right, were still in situ in 2006.

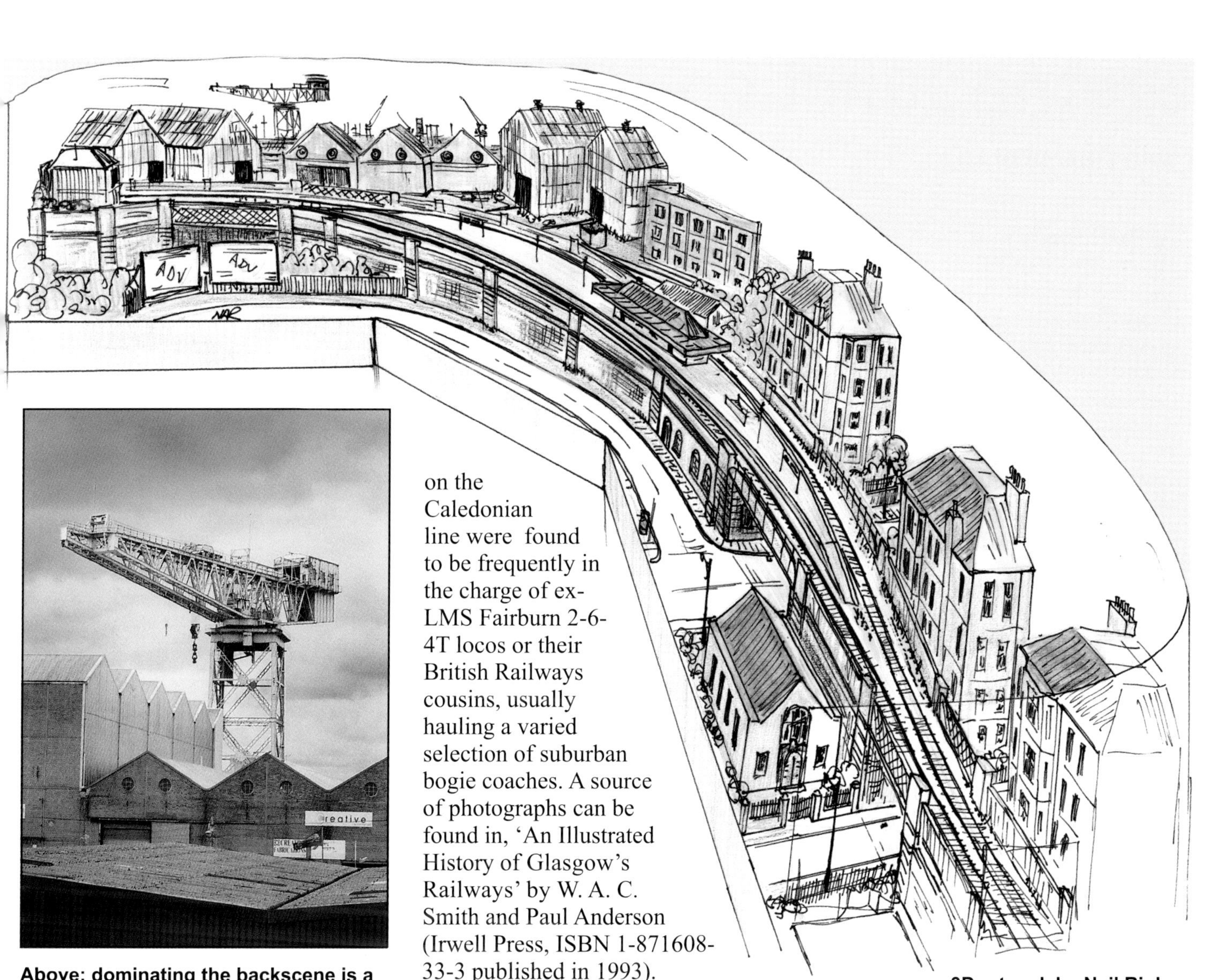

3D artwork by Neil Ripley

Above: dominating the backscene is a shipyard crane, based on this one seen near Whiteinch in 2006.

Below: the chapel featured in the plan is based on this building; Clydebank Baptist Church in Alexander Street as it was in 2006.

on the Caledonian line were found to be frequently in the charge of ex-LMS Fairburn 2-6-4T locos or their British Railways cousins, usually hauling a varied selection of suburban bogie coaches. A source of photographs can be found in, 'An Illustrated History of Glasgow's Railways' by W. A. C. Smith and Paul Anderson (Irwell Press, ISBN 1-871608-33-3 published in 1993).

Such a scene could also be operated during the green diesel period utilising similar rolling stock. The Hornby 06 diesel shunter, or a kit equivalent, would be a good choice, although some other suitable but less common diesel shunter types can be obtained from certain kit manufacturers in 4mm and 7mm scale. The use of the Heljan Class 26 and 27 in BR Green should not be dismissed, whilst their newly released Class 17 Bo-Bo would be a useful addition to the Glasgow or Scottish scene. I have seen photographs of Class 17s hauling suburban passenger trains within Glasgow. Other Scottish 'green liveried' diesels could be utilised too although one or two of the above mentioned classes in rail blue could be introduced especially if they were to be found with their pre-TOPS numbers affixed.

I must conclude by stating that visits to such areas are extremely important as a means to creating the correct atmosphere. I have located some new areas of attraction, and dare I say, they are outside my usual North British spheres of interest: oh, so many ideas, so little time... And the name, *Victoria Yard* this is named after the area in which the project is set, and the station would probably be *Victoria Riverside*. For those interested in such matters, the actual station opposite was called Scotstoun East, and of course the Victoria part comes from the nearby Victoria Park, which is again the fictitious location for my own Glaswegian saga in 7mm. I really do like my 'just supposing' projects to have a reasonably true background.

Gretna Junction

Main line running

Ten miles or so north of Carlisle, actually on the Border itself and close to the Solway Firth, sits the small town of Gretna Green. Not so very long ago, courting couples could run away and get married over the famous blacksmith's anvil, but not anymore.

Here, the railway has run parallel with the A74 since leaving Carlisle, and both road and rail continue to follow the same valleys as they head north towards Glasgow. The line of course, is the old Caledonian Railway route to Glasgow, now electrified and perhaps better known as the West Coast Main Line. There are no Stanier Pacifics to be seen though, these days Pendolinos and Voyagers seem to operate the passenger services, although until quite recently, it was still possible to see the 1960s' AC Electric classes, with 'proper' coaching stock. Some diesel traction is still evident on freight.

However, let us return to Gretna, because situated at this location, on the main line is a simple junction which takes the old Glasgow and South Western line away westwards to Dumfries and eventually northwards to Glasgow via Kilmarnock. No doubt in earlier days, this junction would have had a more elaborate track plan, but only three plain, if quite generous turnouts were to be found there until recently. Over the last decade or so, much track rationalisation has taken

Gretna Junction at a glance

Design Scale:	**4mm, but ideal for reduction to N gauge.**
Location:	**West Coast Main Line just over the Border.**
Period:	**Present day, some scope for backdating.**
Size of Layout:	**8ft x 1ft 6in.**
Motive Power:	**Contemporary stock; Pendolinos, 158, 156 Classes 66, 67.**
Typical Traffic:	**Main line passenger, container trains, general freight trains, cross country passenger trains.**

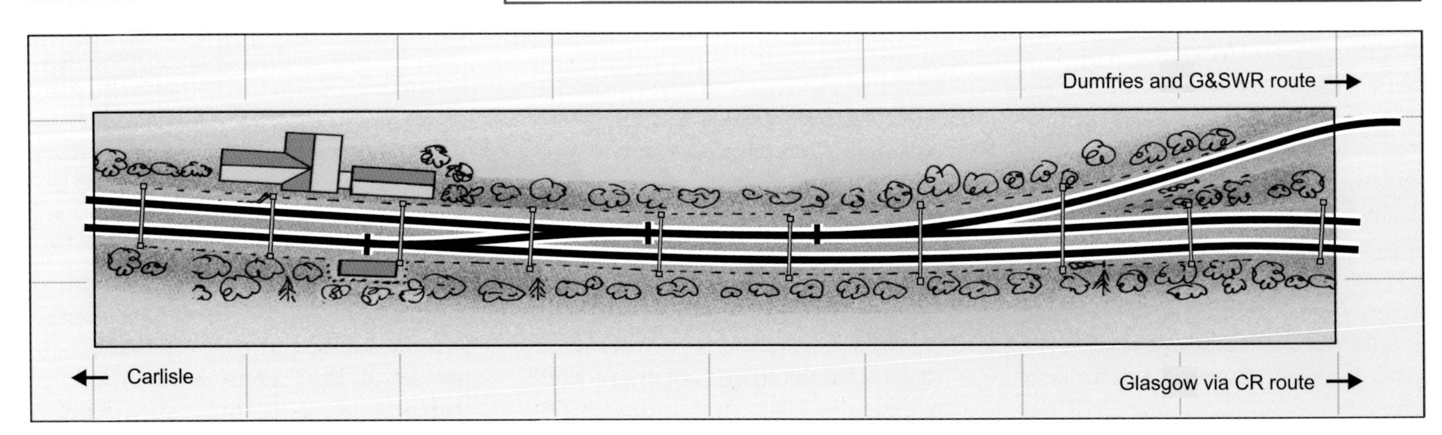

Left: looking north towards the junction. Note the complex assembly of stretchers and locking bars on the high speed turnouts.

Above: the former Gretna (CR) station building is now a private house.

place throughout the network, and no doubt Gretna Junction has received such treatment.

This project can really be as small or as large as you like. Modelling just the junction allows you to have the Pendolinos and Voyagers whizzing by on the main line whilst still allowing a modicum of cross-country type passenger trains and freight originating from the ex-G&SWR branch. Freight services can be quite varied and on a recent visit I did see examples of timber traffic and container services. Ironically coal traffic can also be seen flowing in both directions: heading south from the Hunterston deep water terminal, or north from the new coal facility at Blyth! As a matter of fact, the G&SWR route is often used as a diversionary route when the WCML is closed for engineering works, usually at weekends or during the evening.

I've taken a radical approach with this design: radical for me, that is; and produced the accompanying track plan representing the junction itself. The idea is that this is incorporated into a much expanded layout, with a full compendium of hidden-sidings, filled to the gunnels with passenger and freight workings: should time, space and inclination be available, naturally. Typically this would be on narrow shelf style baseboards and the whole layout could run around a garage or loft room perimeter with the operating positions in the centre.

Another option would be to scale it down to an N gauge layout, though still occupying a similar area to allow longer runs and more hidden sidings directly behind the scenic section. Tight curves could be provided at each end, so the layout could be built on a solid top set of boards, rather than around a central well. The tight curves could easily be hidden out of sight in this instance, at the south end by the overbridge and cuttings and woodland at the junction end.

Despite being extremely close to the town, it is quite a rural location in some ways, with just a few buildings occupying the old site, including the CR style station building complete with crow stepped gables! I feel sure that the site has been like this with a simplified track layout for some years, along with the colour light signals, so equally, it could be backdated to highlight the use of the indomitable BR AC classes. There is the little matter of fitting some overhead catenary of course, but it should not be as difficult as you might imagine, since elements of the European systems from European firms, Viessmann and Sommerfeldt, are suitable for UK outline.

However, with a little research, it would be possible to discover what the junction looked like during the early green or blue diesel periods, before the catenary masts and associated wires became a blot on the landscape, and might I add, the bane of most railway photographers! That would allow the use of the rather nice Hornby Class 50s, usually found double-heading the services up to Glasgow prior to electrification in the mid 1970s.

Whilst researching the junction, Network Rail announced they were to double the trackwork between Gretna and Annan. This would be completed, I assume, sometime after 2008. Interestingly, since writing this section, and in spite of the expense, a new twin-track junction has recently been re-instated here on the West Coast Main Line. So by accident rather than by design, this scheme which was meant to be 'an up-to-date' plan, has turned out to be an historical period one instead!

The accompanying photographs show the old station building of Gretna station (now a private house). The building is very close to the north-bound track so conceivably, should be included. And by the way, the story of me trying to locate the junction one wet February day does not bear thinking about!

Fort William oil depot

An adjunct to a larger layout or a cameo sized project

I am unsure as to when the oil terminal at Fort William was constructed, but I have seen photographs of the small depot in the late steam period. In a previous life, it had been a ballast siding. It still stands to this day and at the time of writing (late 2007) it had been in use once again. It makes an interesting subject for a small 4mm 'micro-style' layout on its own, or as an adjunct to a larger scheme. It has the distinct modelling advantage of being in between two bridges, which creates two scenic breaks! The left hand bridge takes a public road across the railway, whilst the right hand bridge originally carried the British Aluminium Company narrow gauge railway down to the shores of Loch Linnhe.

The oil terminal is found at the end of a short kick back siding close to Fort William Junction just beyond BACo bridge. The track along the front edge runs to Fort William station, a quarter of a mile or so towards town. At either end of the scenic sections small hidden sidings or cassettes will be required, long enough to take the longest train. I would suggest nothing longer than a two car 158, or two coaches and a K3, if set in steam days: anything longer would be unmanageable.

Not shown on the plan, is a further oil storage area (extreme left in the photograph) linked by underground pipelines from the siding. From here, lorries deliver fuel oil throughout the Lochaber area. Including this additional area could be done if the baseboards were made slightly wider.

The rail terminal has security fencing around all sides and a locked gate over the tracks, as seen right. It would be interesting to make this gate work, as the terminal would usually be locked up when not in use.

Within the oil terminal, there are a series of pipe distribution outlets. In 4mm scale, these can be sourced from the Knightwing plastic kits range. In other scales it could be an interesting soldering job using brass tube and etched hand wheels. A small hut or shelter is to be found at the site, easily fabricated from wood or plastic sheet.

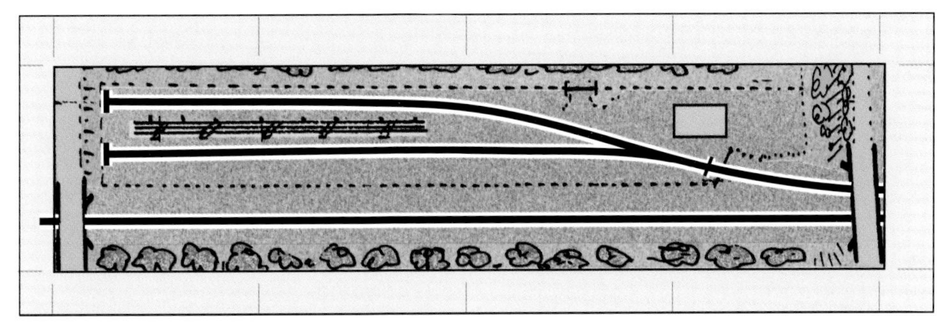

Operation of this small layout is quite simple, the passenger trains shuttle back and forth along the front and the oil terminal sidings would be shunted by the Fort William pilot. In steam days, that could have been one of the three allocated ex-NBR J36 0-6-0s. After that, especially during the 'green diesel' period, a Class 08 was used along with Class 20s. This also happened during the later 'blue' period although once again, I bet one or two Class 27s delivered wagons into the terminal. Even the Class 37s would have probably found their way inside too. Bringing us right up to date, assuming the terminal to be still in use, Class 66s would noisily creak and groan over the trackwork. It might also be a useful introduction to DCC, with locomotive sound; screeching brake blocks and engine noise, and lights of course.

For rolling stock, the traditional 14T tank wagon would still be seen in the 1970s alongside the newer TTAs. A variety of liveries would be seen, although the majority of wagons used would be well and truly weathered!

In conclusion, this small diorama would be yet again ideally suited as an introduction to the finer 4mm scales. With such a small amount of stock required, there would be plenty of time to experiment with some of the modelling challenges associated with finer scale standards. In any case, it would be a most excellent introduction to being involved in matters West Highland.

The Rothbury Branch

A border branch line of the North British Railway

Once upon a time, if you looked beyond the end of the platforms at Rothbury, it was possible to see where the line was intended to continue northwards. Had the Northumberland Central Railway been constructed in its entirety, it would have probably headed over the Border into Scotland. The deposited plans indicated it was to traverse Northumberland from Scotsgap, in the Parish of Hartburn, to the Parish of Ford in north Northumberland, then with a branch across the Border, join up with the NER branch between Berwick upon Tweed and Kelso. In my earlier book, one of the modelling projects was named *Ford Castle*.

From the outset the NCR was beset with difficulties. Despite having received its Act of Parliament in 1863, the building work on the line did not commence until the spring of 1866. The usual financial problems and arguments between directors, shareholders and contractors were the main reasons. Eventually the directors were forced to make a formal application to abandon the route north of Rothbury. As it happens, it was the northern part of the line, which would probably have created the most profit for the company. That part of the line was eventually served by the Cornhill Branch, between Alnwick and Coldstream, and financed by the North Eastern Railway. The greatly truncated Rothbury Branch, as it became known, finally opened to traffic in November 1870. The NBR took over the company in early 1872.

In the end, Rothbury became the only terminus station on the North British Northumbrian branches. In many respects though, it was not a typical example of a small NBR terminus station. For a start, at the very end was a 42ft turntable, which allowed locomotives to either run around their coaches, or access the tiny engine shed. An earlier wooden shed on this site had burnt down in 1915. The station building was also made of wood, but it survived until final closure in November 1963. Lack of finance was once again the main reason why many of the buildings on the Rothbury Branch were constructed of wood. Quite a long platform was provided, complete with the usual grounded body of an old NBR six-wheeled coach being used as a store. At the end of the platform was a sturdy stone built signal cabin behind which were a few sidings which served loading banks and cattle pens. Some carriage sidings were also provided and these proved useful on Rothbury race days or when there was a large cattle market under way. The turntable at the end of the platform was also used to reach some agricultural merchants, whilst a complicated set of turnouts in the middle of the site gave access to the yard and carriage sidings as well as the loop.

Consequently, for a small country terminus, the expanse of trackwork is considerable, and a reasonably accurate model needs a fairly spacious baseboard! However, the beauty of building a model of this fine terminus will be evident from the amount of operation which will be possible when it is completed. As the passenger service ceased in September 1952, I always prefer to model the Border branches circa 1951. By modelling Rothbury during that year, only two locomotives will need to be built.

Ivatt 2MT No. 46474 shunts the goods yard at Rothbury sometime in the late 1950s. Photograph W. S Sellar.

Passenger services were operated with a charming ex-NER G5 0-4-4T locomotive and a non-corridor coach of some vintage whilst the daily freight service utilised the ever hard-working J21 0-6-0 locomotives, also of NER parentage. These ex-NER locomotives worked most of the Northumbrian branch lines since the grouping, along with the occasional NBR 0-6-0, most usually a J36. All of these locomotives are available as kits in 4mm and 7mm scale.

I would suggest therefore, Rothbury would be an ideal candidate for the kit construction enthusiast working in the finer standards of 4mm scale - EM or P4. Locomotive construction could be limited to just two of the classes mentioned above, although some reserve motive power might be warranted. A wide selection of rolling stock could easily be built up from kits, with an emphasis on sourcing a good range of cattle wagons. The standard BR cattle wagon would not really be appropriate, as they would not have been in such widespread use by the early 1950s. However, there are plenty of other 4mm cattle wagon kits on the market. Other specialist vehicles would be horse-boxes, and if one imagined a Rothbury race day service, a fair number of excursions were operated from industrial Tyneside and County Durham. Many of these services would have been hauled along the Rothbury branch with J21s or J25s. Photographs have been published showing the ex-NER J27 locomotives working the branch, though only occurred towards the end of the branch's life in the early 1960s.

For those interested in prototypical operation of a small rural branch line, Rothbury must be a most suitable contender, particularly if you are looking for one with a Scottish flavour. If you back-dated this model into the early 1920s, correct operation of the branch would require a Holmes 'C' Class 0-6-0 (J36) along with the diminutive Drummond 'R' Class 4-4-0 Tank Locomotive (D51), three or four short NBR four or six wheeled coaches and a good selection of pre-grouping rolling stock. Naturally the bulk of these items would need to be scratchbuilt, although an increasing number of such kits are now becoming available in both 4mm and 7mm scales. During the 1920s and 1930s, a F8 2-4-2T locomotive could be found on the Wansbeck and Rothbury lines too.

Also included in this section can be found the track plans of two of the branches' wayside stations. Both Longwitton (originally named Rothley) and Brinkburn fall into the usual Futers' one-or-two turnout Border plans. However, in earlier times, both stations had further sidings, as colliery lines, and in the case of Brinkburn, an aerial ropeway was linked into the sites.

Much of the mineral wealth, on which these Northumbrian branch lines were built, was to be very quickly worked out, in some instances this was very soon after the opening of these characterful routes. However, a small amount of the coal mining and quarry work continued, albeit on a reduced scale. By the 1950s the mineral traffic had long gone and the economics of keeping the line open were being realised by the operating authorities. Closure loomed, especially for the passenger traffic, but freight surprisingly, carried on well into the 1960s, with final closure of the line in 1963. Now you really don't have a reason not to build this layout, do you?

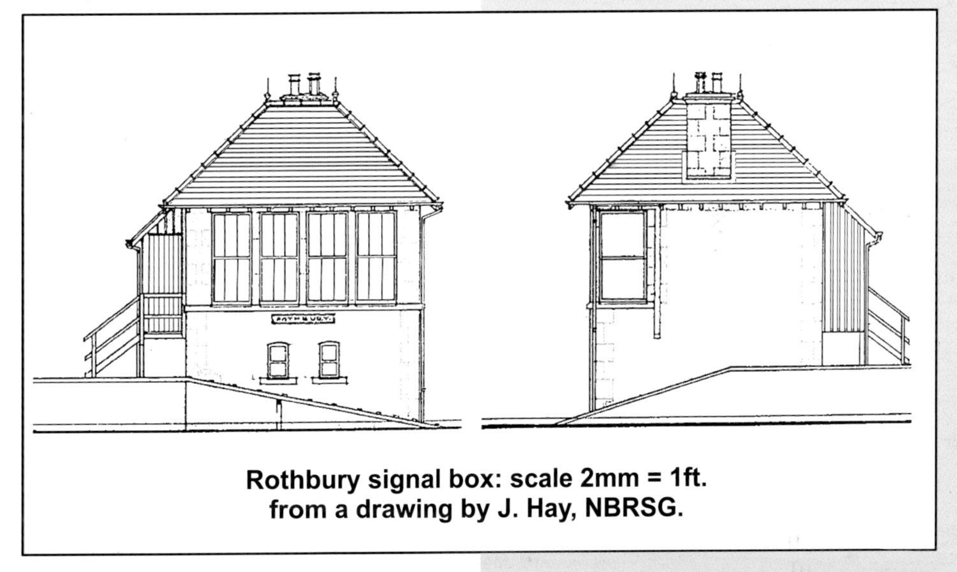

Rothbury signal box: scale 2mm = 1ft. from a drawing by J. Hay, NBRSG.

The Rothbury branch at a glance

Design Scale:	**4mm.**
Location:	**Mid-Northumberland.**
Period:	**Early 1950s.**
Size of Layout:	**See plans overleaf, suitable for a large room.**
Motive Power:	**J21, J25, J27 0-6-0s, G5 0-4-4T, BR Standard Class 2 2-6-0.**
Typical Traffic:	**Branch passenger, general freight, livestock, especially cattle, coal and agricultural produce.**

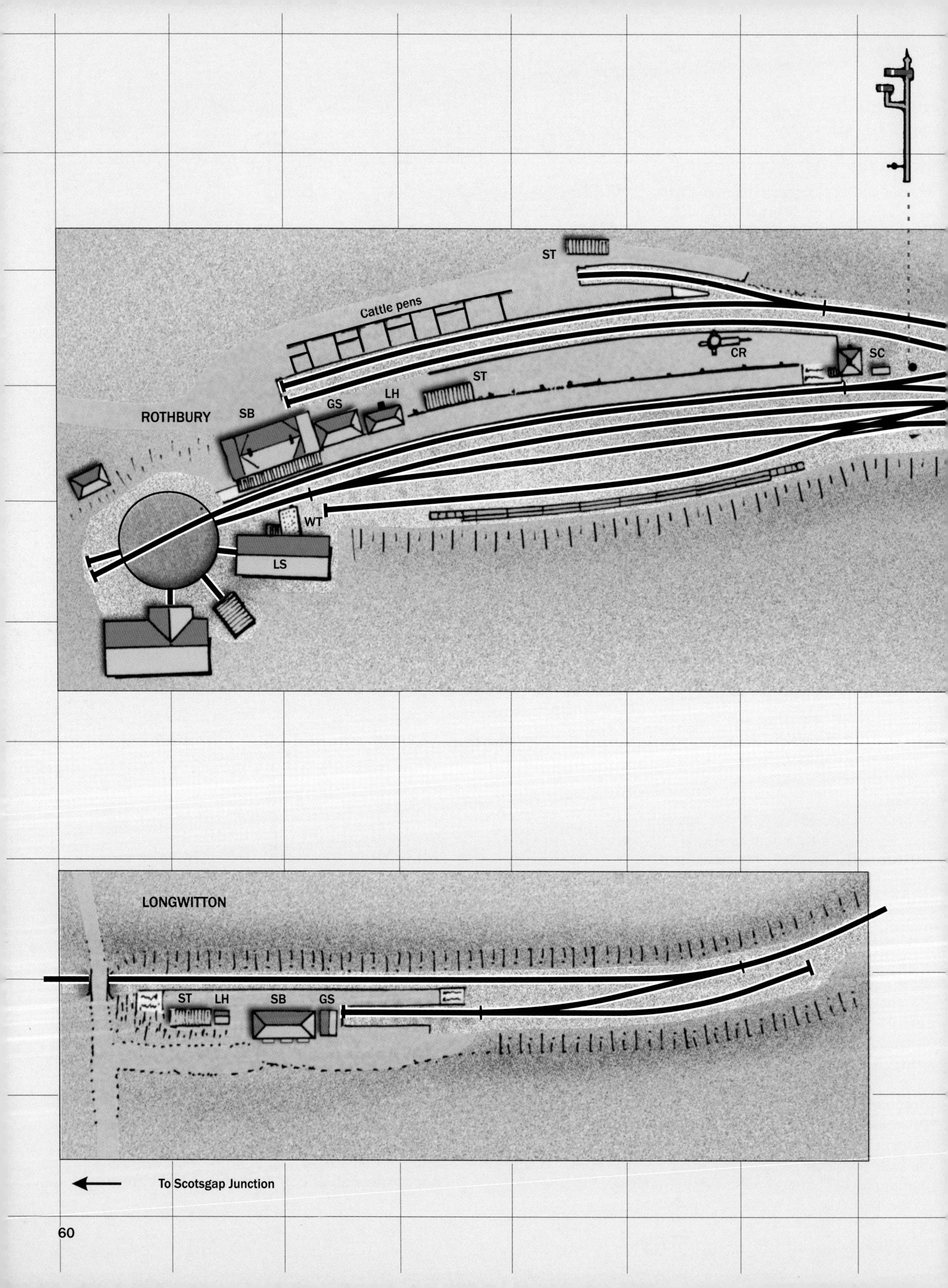
ST
Cattle pens
CR
SC
ST
LH
GS
SB
ROTHBURY
WT
LS
LONGWITTON
ST
LH
SB
GS
To Scotsgap Junction

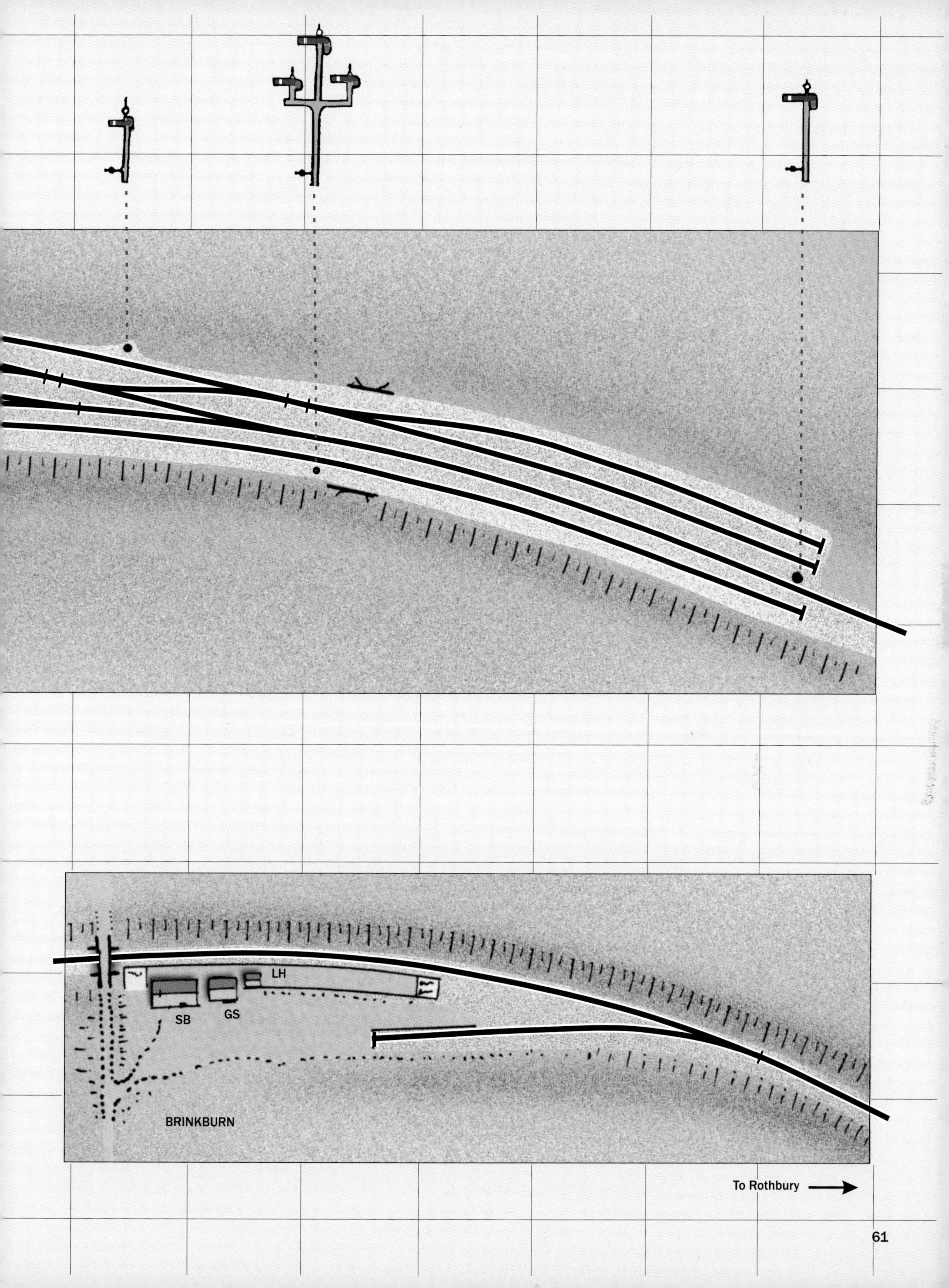
LH
SB
GS
BRINKBURN
To Rothbury

Kielder Forest

A Border Counties' lost oasis

Once again, and as a sort of grand finalé, I return to the Border Counties Railway within Northumberland, but only just! Two and a half miles further up the by now slightly remote North Tyne Valley, we find the single track railway crosses over into Scotland at Deadwater, a station I described in my first book. This part of the Border Counties Railway opened in 1862, the same day that the Waverley Route opened throughout between Edinburgh and Carlisle. The promoters of both routes looked forward to a prosperous period of trade after the considerable expenditure expended upon these routes, much of which was built to counteract the encroachment of the Caledonian Railway and North Eastern Railway companies. The North British Railway wanted a separate route into Newcastle upon Tyne and its own route to Carlisle. The prosperous times took sometime to come, and only occurred when the NBR became partners with the Midland Railway upon the opening of that company's Settle and Carlisle route. This is indeed a valuable lesson for current devotees of the modern idiom, to show that many of the lines operating today had previously led a tangled and sometimes torrid existence in earlier periods. That aside, it does allow such interested parties to follow the history of their chosen routes or prototype and as such, should not be overlooked.

However, back to the Border Counties, which in my humble opinion, is a most agreeable line to model in whatever scale. Kielder Forest has always been my most favourite station on the line: it is compact, only requires five turnouts along with a catch point, but was sometimes used as a passing place within the route as well as a terminus for the service on Saturdays between Kielder and Hexham. Three daily passenger turns passed each way through the station, along with a bonus goods train between Riccarton Junction and Hexham. One or two freights from Edinburgh and Newcastle, were technically speaking, through freights. All in all, the pace of line would have been lethargic rather than Clapham Junction-like. As I will show later on, a dedicated set of coaching stock along with an assortment of freight vehicles are all that is required to operate a totally realistic timetable. Much of the information is readily available from photographs and notes along with the correct locomotive details.

During the 1930s and '40s, the land surrounding Kielder was planted with many trees with most of the saplings coming to Kielder station from Aviemore. Over the years, the landscape became transformed and today, as the trees are maturing and ready to be felled, the Forestry Commission must wish the line was still operational. Indeed the LNER changed the name of the station in the 1940s to Kielder Forest.

The station track plan is contained within a generous curve, in fact the two turnouts into the goods siding are actually 'Y' turnouts. At the end of the nineteenth century, a crossover was installed across the bridge over the Catcleugh Burn and the typical 'Coonties' signal box was installed during this period. The long siding off this crossover was where the saplings were unloaded. The freight siding served not a goods shed, but the more usual stone built loading bank, whilst an infinitesimal kick-back siding from the freight line was deemed to be the

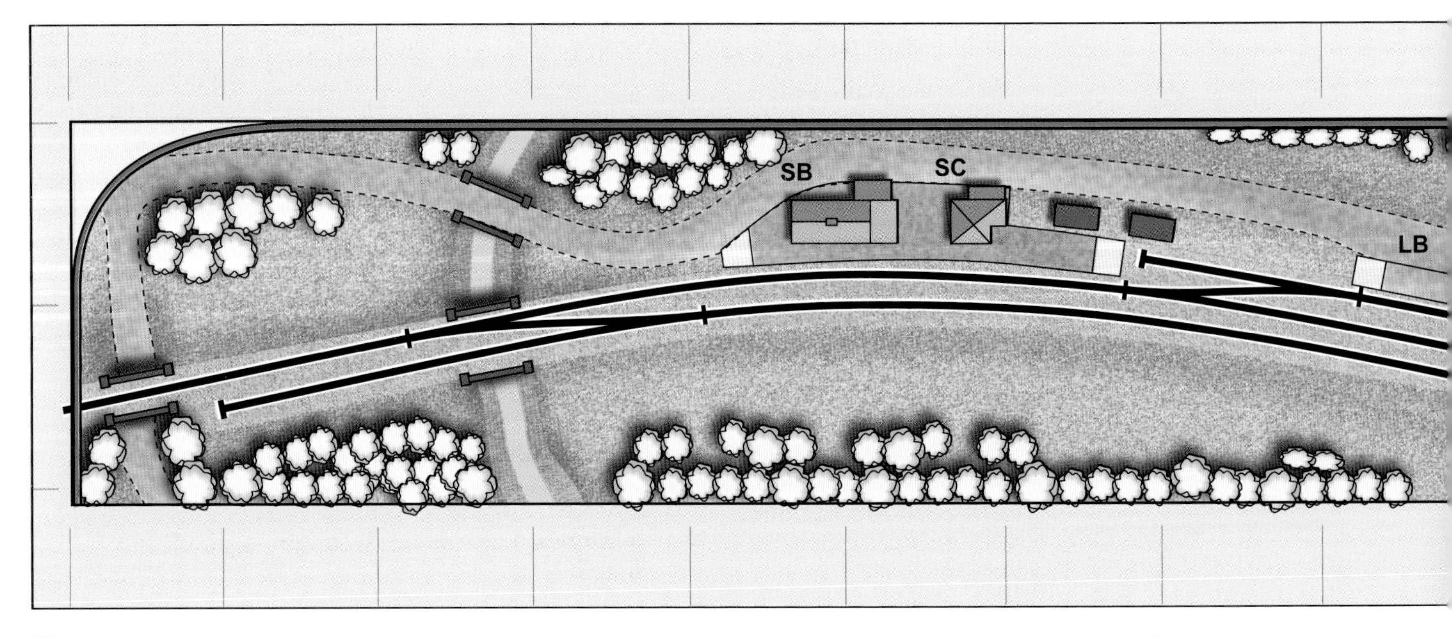

coal siding, although the siding itself could only hold one wagon! At the southern end of the station a single turnout gave access to the main running line and loop, the loop being protected by a catch point. The whole site was signalled with the tall, slender Stevens style lattice post signals so favoured by the NBR and included the same company's flap style ground signals. The NBR arms remained on the line until full closure in 1958.

There was a pair of 'superior cottages', which acted as the station buildings and accommodation for the main station staff. As mentioned above, in about 1896 or so, the atypical signal box was added: they were beautifully constructed in sandstone and today only one example remains, at Wall, close to the junction with the Newcastle and Carlisle route. There was a brick built lamp hut on the platform and a wooden-sleepered shed near to the coal siding. At the opposite end of the site there was a typical NBR platelayers hut which still stands today by the rough track to the Forestry Commission offices. The southern end of the site also had a very convenient road bridge across the tracks, ideal for the characteristic scenic break

With the locomotives and rolling stock now available, mainly as kits, it is quite possible to set the layout within either, the NBR period just before the 1923 Grouping, the LNER period, or the early British Railways period: passenger traffic ceased in October 1956, freight traffic lingered on until 1958. The weak bridge at Border Counties Junction was cited as the reason for closure although the locals will tell you another story. The more likely reason will be linked with poor passenger receipts, though it cannot be denied the line served the isolated communities well for just under a hundred years. The increase in car and lorry ownership after the Second World War probably also assisted the route's demise.

I always prefer the early British Railways era, mainly because I have a lot of operational information regarding that period. Eight NBR 'Scott' class locomotives (Class D30) were allocated to Hawick shed by then, and they hauled much of the traffic over the line. Some larger locomotives appeared right at the end, including B1s, K1s, K3s and the BR Standard classes. Local freight was in the hands of J36s and then J21 0-6-0s. The Saturday Only service between Kielder and Hexham frequently consisted of an ex-Gresley brake composite coach, hauled by a J21 or V3 tank locomotive. For 4mm scale the GEM 'Scott' and 'Glen' kits are still available and would be an ideal introduction to the dying art of white-metal kit construction. The GEM J36 is still be available too, as are the Nu-Cast/Dave Alexander J21 kits. In 7mm scale, practically all the kits are now available including the 'Scott' and 'Glen' kits from NB Models. Further North British prototypes are available in kit form from Connoisseur Models under their Claymore Kits label. No excuses for not operating the correct locomotives.

The same can be said about the coaching stock in both 4mm and 7mm, as kits are available from the old Ian Kirk range (4mm are now sold under a different name). To operate the two coaching rakes: the first; with Gresley non-corridor coaches consisted of a three-compartment brake third, an eight-compartment third or composite, plus a five-compartment brake third. Sometimes a Thompson composite non-corridor would be substituted. The other train, introduced in about 1952, consisted of three Thompson mainline style steel sided coaches in blood and custard livery; a brake composite with a brake third had a third compartment coach sandwiched between them. On occasions, full brake coaches or parcels stock of some vintage would be included into the consists, whilst the odd meat van could also be added.

The usual assortment of wagons and vans, including some pre-grouping stock can also be easily built up from

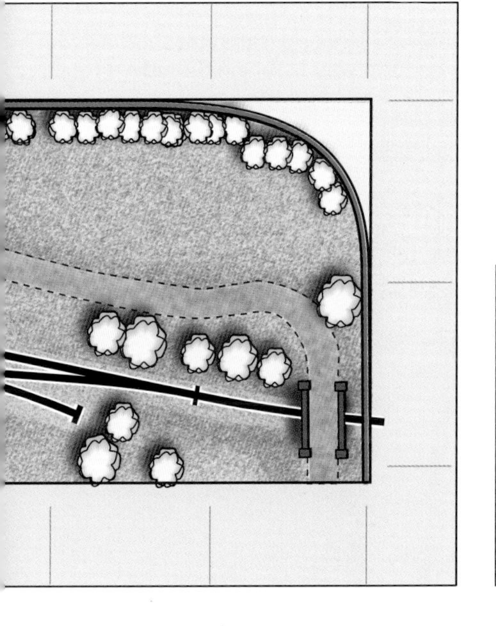

Kielder Forest at a glance

Design Scale:	**4mm, again suitable for other scales.**
Location:	**North west Northumberland, east of Riccarton.**
Period:	**1950s.**
Size of Layout:	**12ft x 2ft 2ins, though scope for compression.**
Motive Power:	**See main text.**
Typical Traffic:	**Branch passenger, general merchandise, livestock, coal, through freight, agricultural produce.**

ready-to-run purchases or alternatively some kit-built models can be built up over time. With this project, you also get a typical day's working timetable, in this case a Saturday, so you can include the Hexham-Kielder service, which has to wait in the loop at Kielder in order to allow another service to cross, before it can amble leisurely back down the North Tyne Valley taking the local residents for shopping or pleasure into Hexham. It would return from Hexham, usually around 9:30 at night, which meant some of the passengers could enjoy an evening at the Forum: the local 'flicks' in Hexham. Its arrival at Kielder was around midnight, the crew had then to bring the locomotive back to Hexham shed, a very long shift from all accounts.

For obvious reasons, the 4mm plan is drawn for a continuous run layout where there would be hidden curves to a small ladder of hidden sidings at the back. If tackled in 7mm scale, I would consider two separate sets of hidden sidings, one at each end of the layout. Either way, the desolate but heavily forested landscape would be interesting to model, and a first, as the natural beauty of the North Tyne valley has been much neglected by modellers over the years. It just so happens I have the station baseboards already constructed for Kielder Forest in 7mm: dare I say 'watch this space'?

The Border Counties line closed to passenger traffic on 15 October 1956, and to freight, for most of the route, on 31 August 1958. Bellingham station remained open for freight, which was operated from Morpeth over the Wansbeck line and Reedsmouth Junction until 11 November 1958. After this time, the service was cut back to Woodburn, which lasted until 3 October 1966.

As a sort of Postscript to this project, every now and again there are reports that the 'operating companies' would like to re-lay the southern part of the Waverley Route from Carlisle up to Riccarton Junction and then along the old Border Counties route to Kielder. This is in order to remove the vast quantities of timber from the forests by rail. I would be delighted if such a project ever came to fruition, but knowing how long these planning applications take, I am hesitating before holding my breath.

Also, towards the end of 2006, the local newspaper; The Hexham Courant, led with an article about a tourist style railway from Kielder southwards for two or so miles. It was to be operated with a wood burning locomotive (naturally!) and three bogie coaches. The line would be narrow gauge and the idea is to link up with cycle paths and walking trails. The trains would carry bicycles and cater for tourists and walkers. The plan seems well thought out, but only time will tell if such a venture will be constructed and last the course: holding one's breath time again!

Locomotive allocations at Hawick Shed (64G) in the 1950s

D30 Scott Class:

62420	Dominie Sampson
62422	Caleb Balderstone
62423	Dugald Dalgetty
62425	Ellangowan
62428	The Talisman
62432	Quentin Durward
62435	Norna
62440	Wandering Willie

The passenger duties on the Border Counties line were frequently shared with two D49 4-4-0s shedded at Blaydon Shed (52C):

D49	62747	The Percy
D49	62771	The Rufford

Other locomotive classes used up until closure included:

B1
K1
K3
J39
D34 'Glen'
BR Std 4MT
BR Std Tank 4MT
LMS 4MT
J36
D20
V1/3
D11
J21

Not a 'Scott' class, but a D33 modified from an old GEM 'Glen' Class D34. Examples could well have operated through Kielder along with the classes mentioned in the sidebar. The model is well over 30 years old and a long way from even modern ready-to-run standards, but as a tailpiece to this book, it brings us back almost full circle to where it all began...